The Custard Apple Tree

for Catherine, I hope this book which I wrote as a love letter to this world is a reminder to walk this earth with a gentle touch,
♡ Lots of love

Rafy Zufur

The Custard Apple Tree

a Novel

by Rafiqa Zubair

Life Rattle Press
Toronto, Canada

The Custard Apple Tree

Copyright 2022 © Rafiqa Zubair

All rights reserved. No part of this book may be reproduced, distributed or transmitted in any form or any means, including photocopying, recording, or other electronic or mechanical methods, without written permission of the copyright owner except for the use of quotations in a book review.

Library Archives Canada Cataloguing in Publications

Life Rattle Press New Writers Series
ISSN 1713 8981

First Canadian Edition
ISBN 978-1-989861-51-6

Cover design by Rafiqa Zubair
Painting on the cover by Raja Ravi Varma titled
The Milk Maid
Copyedited by Kriti Upreti
Typeset by Rafiqa Zubair

Published in Canada by Life Rattle Press
196 Crawford, Street
Toronto, Ontario M6J 2V6
www.liferattle.ca

To Mama and Baba
I am everything and nothing from your existence.

This story is a work of fiction based on real events; however, some characters and events are purely fiction.

Let's not be divided by race, language or religion and walk the earth with a gentle touch.

No nation can ever be worthy of its existence that cannot take its women along with the men. No struggle can ever succeed without women participating side by side with men. There are two powers in the world; one is the sword and the other is the pen. There is a great competition and rivalry between the two. There is a third power stronger than both, that of the women.

- Quaid-E-Azam Muhammad Ali Jinnah,
Founder of Pakistan

Preface

This is my grandmother's story. In 1947, India was split into two parts: the Hindu-majority India and Muslim-majority Pakistan. Zahida Begum, a seventeen-year-old girl, left her hometown of Jabalpur and travelled to Karachi. She settled in Karachi which served as the immigrant city for Indian Muslims in Pakistan. The partition of India displaced fourteen million people and led to two million recorded deaths. My grandmother is now ninety years old and a survivor of this tragedy.

The Present

Karachi, Pakistan
Year 1951
Five Years After the Partition

Chapter One
The Dream

A blanket of snow. I have never seen snow, but I imagine the events of my current life to resemble it. The snow drapes over endless rolling hills for miles. I stand alone amidst it sinking into the world. The icy air gushes every ounce of blood from my heart to my limbs. My body works twice as hard to keep me alive. It fights for me without my request. I don't want to fight anymore. But my muscles shiver, teeth chatter and I fall into a rhythmic movement to generate heat and I survive. For five years now I was simply surviving.

The large blue sign reads "Delhi Junction Station" in white ink. The train station is empty apart from a dull moon that hangs low in the night sky. It's a crescent moon, like the one on the Pakistani flag. A fog seeps into the platform and the eerie hooting of owls disturbs the silence. Abu, my father, sits at an old wooden bench staring down at his hands. His neck appears loose and lifeless.

Abu's white *shalwar kameez* is drenched with sweat, leaving a pale yellow stain. The long sleeve cotton shirt falls to his knees. Abu wears matching harem pants that cinch at his ankles. He yanks the black coat off of his kameez a dressing style adapted by Indian Muslims from the British.

Dried blood and grime sit underneath his nail beds. His hands are mere bones laced with webs of puffy veins and covered with paper skin. Abu's hands were always sturdy; as a child I wrapped my hand around his pointer finger when we explored the bustling markets of Jabalpur on hot summer afternoons.

"Abu *Jaan* are you okay?" My voice muffles as if I am speaking under water. "What's wrong, tell me!"

He doesn't flinch at my shouting.

"Can you hear me Abu? Abu. You need to hear me," I yell louder. The back of my throat throbs.

I lift my hand to cover my eyes. Two sharp lights appear on the tracks. The screeching of the train clashes with my voice.

"Abu, that's our train! It's here, we have to go," I cry out.

The train's powerful engine makes a full stop, and the machine sends grey fumes into the dark.

"Delhi to Mirpurkhas Pakistan. Last train. Delhi to Mirpurkhas Pakistan. Last train," the conductor calls.

It's our train. Our train to Pakistan. We have to go now. Abu gets up from the bench and limps away. His back slouches and he fades into the fog.

"Abu, come back. Our train....It's leaving. Where are Ami, Dadi, and Banu? Are they on the train already? Where is everyone?"

The conductor's voice is deafening. He yells the announcement on loop. The owls hoot constantly; there must be hundreds of them watching us from behind the walls of the abandoned station. I see a pair of chartreuse yellow eyes lurking at Abu from the thick fog. My ears ring and my vision blurs. Abu limps farther away. The more I chase him, the more his silhouette fades away.

I catch up to him after what feels like miles of sprinting. I tug on the corner of his white dirty kameez like I used to as a little girl. Tears burn my cheeks.

"Abu, we have to go...now," I plead through sniffles.

Abu whips his head back. He glares at me. His eyes are bloodshot red, piercing and cold. They reach an unknown place within me and my stomach churns. I drop his kameez and it falls down to his knees.

I fall back. I fall into water. It's too thick to be water.

It's blood.

Thick blood. The stench bleeds into my nose; metal and rotting corpses. Abu stares at me. His lips move but his eyes stay hard like glass. Suddenly they shatter.

"This is the cost of our freedom, Zahida," Abu says and vanishes into a cloud of dust.

I shudder out of a deep sleep. I sit up and run my fingers through my hair pushing it back and out of my face. *It was just a dream. It was just a dream. A horrible nightmare and nothing more.* Remember what Dadi used to teach us; dreams are just tricks of the devil. Don't let the devil play with your mind by believing its foolish tricks. I wish she was here tonight to pray on me and let me nestle into her bed.

I place my hand over my chest. Air reaches my lungs in short takes. I use the end of my white *dupatta* to wipe cold beads of sweat from my forehead. They are replaced by another line of beads dripping from my thick black curls.

A chilly morning breeze comes in through the tears in the fabric covering our hut. The breeze meets the sweat on my damp body and a shiver runs down my spine. I bring the shawl up to my neck. It's my mother's shawl; a beautiful brown embroidered with fine red flowers. It doesn't smell like her anymore. It doesn't smell like jasmine flowers. It doesn't smell like a fresh mix of spices from our kitchen; cardamom, cinnamon, and turmeric.

I bury my tired face into it anyways.

Through the fine threads I can see dawn creeping in. A soft sunlight seeps through the dark fabrics that we call our walls. I lay there letting the sunlight trickle through the shawl onto my face absorbing its warmth. I lay there hoping this reality is another nightmare and I will wake up at home. Our real home. I lay there missing the walls, the marble, and the custard apple trees. It all seems like a distant memory now; like re-reading a letter so many times it loses the voice of its writer and all that remains are hollow words that have no use being missed.

The mullah of the small community of Lalu Khet sings the morning call to prayer.

> *God is Great! God is Great!*
> *I bear witness that there is no God,*
> *except the One God.*
> *I bear witness that Muhammad is*
> *the messenger of God.*
> *Hurry to the prayer. Hurry to salvation.*
> *God is Great! God is Great!*

The soulful melody sinks into every hut for miles. The prayer wakes up every able-bodied man and woman to start another day of hard work to build Pakistan. I drape my white dupatta over my black curls and crawl out of the woven straw bed. The earth beneath the straw mat lets the cold seep into my bare feet.

I slip on my black sandals. The strap of one sandal comes loose but I tuck it back into place. Out of the clay pot I dish out a steel glass of chilled water; the glass comes out half full.

I step out into the community. The fiery morning sun droops low in the sky and a heavy dreadful air halos over the barren land upon which thousands of huts sit. The huts house thousands of immigrant families. They are built out of anything and everything; old broom sticks, scraps of wood, torn sheets, *saris*, and toxic metals. No one here can afford cement or low-quality clay to build real walls. Like Abu's hands in my dream, this sight looks too wrong and empty to be called a community.

Ours is on top of the hillier end of the sand

dunes. Rows and rows of huts wrapped with all sorts of colorful old fabrics sit on dry unfertile land. Each barley takes up little squares of earth. They are like little dots randomly scattered on an empty map. Pakistan was an idea on a map. For the Muslim League leaders it was a line that they drew, but for the rest of us it was our lives that they jeopardized. But change doesn't come without the power of people. Here we were making Pakistan what it was supposed to be; a nation.

The endless Sindh desert stretches across the community with not even a tree in sight. Little flags of Pakistan soar high above most of the huts. The green flag with its white crescent moon and star contrasts against the bleak dirty reds, browns, and greys of the huts. The orange light makes the community look like something out of a British newspaper with the headline:

INDIAN MUSLIM IMMIGRANTS LIVE IN
TENTS IN THE PROMISING PAKISTAN

⌣

I stroll with two large steel pots underneath

my arms through small alleyways that reek of piss, dung and disappointment. Children in shredded clothes have already started the begging of the day and men wander unemployed. The women stir large pots of porridge and lentils over open fires. Meat is scarce in these parts. My mouth waters at the thought of lamb korma, chicken biryani or even roasted fish that I would have curled my nose at before.

I spot Zubair Chacha at the end of the fourth alleyway from our hut. He's an elderly man in his sixties. He helped us secure a hut when we first arrived at the community with nothing but nine hungry mouths, a handful of rupees, and hopeful hearts. Zubair Chacha was a soldier in India and fought beside the British in the Second World War. He was against betraying India when the idea of Pakistan was first proposed, but being a Muslim was treacherous enough. He lost his position and the support of his Hindu friends forcing him to leave. I approach him as he sits on a broken wooden stool rinsing his mouth with water and using his finger to brush his teeth.

"Salam Chacha."

"What chore are you off to today, Zahida?" He asks.

I lift my pots.

"Water. It's gone before the evening prayer these days in our hut. I thought I'd get a head start to beat the line up. You know how crowded it gets before the Friday prayer. I think they said something last Friday about not delivering water on the weekends. Are you taking a day off today?"

Lalu Khet's water is brought by a few guys every morning with a tanker truck. The truck stays there for a few hours before it makes rounds to the other communities.

"It's Friday already? No, I am not taking a day off I must just be getting old. Let me grab my pots and I'll come with you." He slips into his tent.

The whole community will be awake in a few hours and march with their pots to get the day's water. They will march as an army marches. That's what we all had done. Some of us walked, some took trains and flights to our own trenches for a dream. But this was the reality of war and the cost of dreaming.

Zubair Chacha appears from behind the grey drapes of his hut. He hangs two strings each with more than a dozen pots over his shoulder. His back arches. His back stayed arched long after the day was over and the loads of water were delivered. It isn't a job fitting for a man who fought in the trenches of Europe and was gloated upon his return to the country. But having fought for the British was nothing to be proud of here. Water, although happened to be just as prestigious and valued. Alongside a small day wage, he received blessings from men, women and their children. Zubair Chacha gained a reputation around the whole community. Small disputes were reported to him and the community asked him for advice.

Zubair Chacha's *lungi* drags on the muddy pathways. His white tank top has small tears along the bottom. He is from southern India; the region of Madras. There was a bit of every part of India here. We walk together now.

"Your henna darkened." He examines the round circle on my palm.

The Custard Apple Tree

I move my hand behind my thighs.

"Yeah, it is darkening."

"Nervous? Every girl is nervous before her wedding. It's normal. You know my sisters? When the eldest was getting married, she was so nervous that she could barely keep down a meal a whole week before her *nikah*. God keep them all well wherever they are now."

I never ask him about his family. One day I was at the community's restrooms when I heard two women talking.

"You know I was on the same train as Zubair. It was going from Madras to Delhi," a women wearing a shiny yellow sari said.

I never had an ear for gossip, but the woman's tone was serious.

"His youngest sister was my age. I was friends with her." The women's voices collided with the squeaky taps as they filled up their small toilet pots.

"Really?" The shorter woman responded.

"Yeah, she was in her forties."

"Where are they now? He sure talks about them a lot."

"They are dead," the woman in the yellow

sari said.

I remember gasping.

"Dead, what do you mean?"

"The train went up in flames, my own family barely escaped. I am from the same village as Zubair. I saw him come out of the fire, alone."

"Alone? How could he do that to his sisters?" The shorter woman asked.

"That's why he talks so much about them. He tells himself they escaped too for the sake of his sanity. That guilt weighs down his shoulders."

I rushed out of the stuffy stall, gasping for air.

"Zahida *beti*, I didn't mean to sadden you by asking you about your henna." Zubair Chacha interrupts the long silence.

"Oh no Chacha, I am not sad that you asked. I was just thinking about something," I mutter. The rest of our words hover over us in hot clouds of sand and dust. We all have a lot of words, but no one speaks. No one mentions how awful things are. How bankers, soldiers and doctors sleep homeless and how the facade of hope has worn off in the long years. But I have to speak now.

I turn to him and ask, "Chacha, who will get the water for all my siblings?"

"I make runs for water everyday, what's one more hut?" A shame creeps in on me. I feel small. I never knew what it felt like to be in the shoes of the poor. I never realized how much pride it took away from a person. I lower my head.

"I can't afford to pay you. All the money from my tutoring is going into Banu, Majid and Abid's schooling." I gaze far away where the water tank starts to become visible.

"I don't want them on these streets, Chacha. They will get sucked into it all. You see the kids stealing, doing shameless things like drugs, and everything else but getting an education. The space inside that hut is the only safe place for them. And, I will be married. Married and..."

He knew my pride would be hurt if he pitied me.

"What if I made you a deal?"

My lips curl up into a smile.

"Clean water deliveries every morning to your siblings and every time you come home you make me that delicious rice pudding?" He says.

"How about every *Jummah*?"

"Every Friday it is. That's a done deal."

That's one worry off my shoulders.

The sun lingers over us and the heat burns my back. I stare down at the circle on my palm. The earthy red stain glows against my pale skin. Like the circle on my palm another thought plays on loop; *I will be a married woman and both my parents are dead.*

Chapter Two
Barfi

The kitten scratches the end of my dupatta with its claws.

"No, not another one Banu," I say.

"But *Api*, please. It's just a little cat. It's just one more little mouth to feed. Pleeeease." She whines.

"One more mouth. Stale bread and watery tea for dinner aren't even enough for our stomachs. You want me to say yes right now and then have this thing starve and die under my name. I don't want its ill wishes," I reply.

"She has a name you know. She's not a thing. Her name is Barfi." The white kitten pouts at me. Banu has the same stupid pout on her face.

"Fine! But I am not taking care of her or feeding her."

"Thank you, thank you so much Api. I love you." Banu lunges forward to hug me. She pinches my cheeks and dashes away with her kitten.

"Banu, come back here!" I shout.

She's getting older. Her straight black hair flows down her back. I miss the days when my own hair wasn't brittle. I am only twenty-two years old, but my face says otherwise. My cuticles have tiny callouses from scrubbing pots and pans all day. My fair skin is burned and peels like garlic from the long afternoons spent walking under the sun from one local school to another.

But I protect Banu. I don't let the sun burn her pretty milky skin, or let her hair become dry. I give free tuition lessons to whoever is willing to take them. I trade my skill of teaching for small bowls of curd and coconut oil. Once a week, I sit Banu down just like Ami would sit us down and rub oil into her hair and yogurt where her skin is dry. She tells me everything and by the end when her hair is braided, both our burdened hearts feel lighter. I cherish these moments with my little sister. We both know it's only a matter of time before our faiths part us from each other forever.

She brings home any hungry strays that pout at her. Children, dogs with fleas, birds with broken wings, and now this fluffy white kitten. Barfi follows her around everywhere. At night when I shoo her away, she curls up outside of our tent. And when I wake up in the morning to grab the days water, she meows at me for a morning meal. I know better than to waste precious food on a hungry kitten.

But Banu doesn't know the value of money or food yet. When we all sit down to eat dinner, she feeds the kitten almost half of her roti. So, I start yawning and backing away from my full plate.

"What's wrong?" Banu asks.

"Nothing I am just so full from lunch. I can't even look at this food. The other teachers at the school always bring us lunch."

As I clear my roti off my plate, Banu grabs it.

"I don't want it to go to waste," she explains.

My stomach growls as I wash the night's dishes. But when I peer over and hear Banu's restful snores, I feel the strength I need to get through another day. I have to keep surviving for them.

Chapter Three
The Indian Empire

The year of the partition was 1947. The Second World War had just ended. Britain was bankrupt. The Indian empire had fallen back in the hands of India itself. There was no empire. The times of kings had long gone and everywhere around the world, empires fell to the faith of democracy. The New World was one of the people.

A democratic India emerged. An India made of the people by the people. The country was built up of three main religions with two as the majority in the order of: Hinduism, Islam, and Sikhism. Should India go back to the Muslims or the Hindus? The roaring question became a steamy discussion in every newspaper, radio, and alleyway.

Two political parties forged: the Indian National Congress Party and The Muslim League. The Indian National Congress Party was led by Mahatma Gandhi who believed in a unified India where everyone would live in peace as they had been. The leader of the Muslim League Party, Qaida-A-Azam Muhammad Ali Jinnah vouched for two separate nations; two independent countries, one for the Muslim and one for the Hindus and Sikhs. It was a war on religion and everyone with even an ounce of faith was forced to have an opinion.

A fire of ideas spread through the nation at schools, workplaces and on the bustling streets of the old country. *And chaos was unleashed.*

The Past

Jabalpur, India
Year 1946
One Year Before the Partition

Chapter Four
Last Day

It was the last day. Had I known that my life would change forever after that day, I would have cherished it more.

"Why do I have to wear these, Ami?" I struggled to put on the fancy new gold anklets. The bells dug into my soft skin.

"Because I said so." My mother's voice was stern.

"But Banu doesn't have to wear them," I snickered.

"Banu is still young. You are the eldest daughter. You have to start looking like a proper lady now," Ami said.

"I do look like a lady. What does being a lady have to do with wearing bells around your feet like a cow on Eid?" I rolled my eyes.

Eid was my favourite holiday. The whole mansion was lit with string lights for days before the actual holiday. The days building up to the holiday consisted of trips to the markets to choose an animal for the sacrifice and shopping for the most elaborate dresses. In the late afternoons leading up the festival I took the cow on long walks with Abu, parading it through different neighborhoods before the sun set and the golden city of Jabalpur twinkled into a long evening. I never let any of the poor kids who ran after us touch the cow. I would lift my chin and dust off the areas where they tried to pet the cow.

Jabalpur never saw dark. When the Muslim festivals ended the Hindu festivities began. Even on the coldest winter nights the city was warm with people, music, and lights.

Ami massaged coconut oil into my long black curls as I fastened both the anklets. The fine gold picked up the chandelier light, making it glimmer. And suddenly I loved those anklets even though they pierced my skin. I showed them off at school for the rest of that week. I adjusted the cuffs of my shalwar in front of all the other girls. I came from one of the richest families in Jabalpur and I found pride in that. My father was a merchant. Our fabrics were exported as far as Turkey and the holy city of Medina.

Ami brushed my hair with a wooden comb and braided it down my back. The thick braid dangled with perfect curls glazed in coconut oil. Ami stood in front of the large wooden framed mirror and repeated the process with her own hair. The wooden frame had the finest detail carvings of roses with their thorns. It was imported from Delhi. Abu handpicked it on one of his trips there.

He always brought back gifts for my mother and us, even though she never asked for anything but his safe return. I on the other hand made a list of things for him to bring back the night before his trips. When he came home, I unpacked his suitcase throwing things left and right to dig out my presents.

"You really need to teach this girl some patience!" Ami yelled.

The Custard Apple Tree

"She's just an excited child," Abu said.

"No, she is spoiled. There is a difference between being a grateful child and being spoiled," Ami argued.

I didn't think I was spoiled. Abu worked hard to make us happy. He worked hard for the life we lived, the least I could do was enjoy it.

When Abu left for his trips, Ami wrapped a blessed black bracelet of seven knotted threads on Abu's wrist. Then he whispered in Ami's ear if she wanted anything from the trip. She looked down, smiled and shook her head.

"Just come back in one piece and please take care of yourself," Ami ordered.

"Watch the home while I am gone. Call for Ram if you need anything. I told him to make rounds every day but call for him if you need anything."

"I will. Be safe," Ami said.

He turned to all of us one by one, giving us kisses and hugs. Then finally it was my turn.

"I picked out a few books from my study and set them aside. I want you to read all of them and before you're done, I'll be back with a suitcase full of more books for you to read." He pinched the tip of my nose.

"I am getting faster and faster at reading Abu, you better shorten your trip," I teased.

"Take care of your Ami, will you, look at her already. Oh, my Kurash Jaan! You will get sick if you cry like this."

Ami was indeed sick. Abu had taken her to many *hakeems*, but they couldn't come up with a diagnosis. Some nights her body would go ice cold and she vomited fresh blood. Some days all she could do was lay down and rest.

Abu was right, Ami needed to stay happy to stay healthy. I tugged at her arm, laced my fingers into hers and nudged her.

"My *pyari* Ami don't cry or else Abu will be worried for the rest of his trip," I comforted.

"Now Kurash do you want me to be worried?" Abu asked.

Not being able to make out words, she looked down, pressed the end of sari into her eyes with tears flowing steadily and shook her head. Abu never left until she stopped crying. We made jokes. Banu wiped Ami's tears with her small hands until Ami finally stopped crying and we were all laughing.

We watched as Abu got onto a horse carriage with steel suitcases and tiffins packed with his favourite meal for the trip. He waved and she turned away wiping her tears with the end of her sari.

Banu ran after his carriage. I always stayed by Ami's side.

"He will be back, Ami. Please, you know he's right, you will get sick," I said.

"I know. I'll just miss him."

"I know, me too but he will be back."

Ami knew he would always come back. But for the days he was gone her glance stayed fixated at the front door with every task she did. Her eyes stared at the marble steps until he arrived, sometimes within days and other times months later.

Ami said love was respect. I never heard her say Abu's name; Syed Murad Ali. She referred to him as our father, but he was much more than that to her. He was the meals she cooked in the kitchen, the color of the dress she picked to wear in the morning and the last sentence to her every prayer.

Ami planted white jasmine flowers in her hair. Abu left the flowers on their vanity every morning before she woke up. He picked them from our garden.

I spent most of my childhood in our garden. Throughout the entire year it bloomed with life. The acres of land were lined with rows and rows of fruit trees. The wooden fence around it was laced with jasmine flowers. Pink rose and purple lavender bushes bordered the perimeter of the garden. In the middle was the shrine of two Sufi mystic souls. The graves were covered with fancy black velvet blankets. Dadi placed a fresh bed of roses over the velvet blankets every Friday.

My favourite trees were the custard apple trees. During the winter season the trees bloomed with hundreds of green custard apples. The low trees almost stooped down to the ground. Zahid and I spent most of the winters climbing the branches. Zahid filled his pockets with tamarinds, guava, mulberries, black plums and custard apples. Our hands were left sticky, and our shirts stained from the fruits as we stayed in our trees, eating, giggling, and reading. I read everything to him. Zahid was only three years younger, so he listened and understood. He asked me questions and I took joy in answering and explaining. I wanted everything I couldn't have as a girl for him. I wanted him to go to the universities in Delhi and become a writer. I wanted him to come back and teach me everything he would learn.

I stayed hidden with my brother in the treetops reading Shakespeare, Rumi and Ghalib until the evenings when Ami came finding us with a large spoon. Ami scolded me for spending another day with my face buried in a book instead of over a pot learning to cook. We had maids and servants. But I still needed to learn how to cook. I hated cooking and cleaning. I hated doing anything we had appointed maids for. I wanted to have a life with more purpose than the life Ami lived.
I watched as Ami twirled the rope of flowers into a band. Out of the band of white flowers flowed a thick black braid which fell down to

where her dark skin was exposed in her *sari* blouse. She looked like the Hindu Goddesses that were paraded through the city square at the start of Diwali. I spent the five days playing with Bhavna through the city. Her father, Abu's best friend Ram Kaka bought us sugary sweets and small clay pots of warm honeyed milk.

Then after the hot sun set over the low hills of Jabalpur Ram Kaka and Abu sat for hours at the chai hotel discussing how the festival could have been better and the faults of the Hindu priests and mullahs. Abu was not involved in the mosque; he never prayed or recited the Quran. But he watched us children read the Quran every evening in the courtyard and listened with a respectful ear while snacking on roasted peanuts.

"Zahida, put on your gold bangles," Ami ordered as she slipped shiny yellow gold bangles onto her dark slender wrists. Her dull pink sari was pleated neatly like always. A dainty gold chain fell around her swan neck and gold earrings twinkled in her ears.

The Custard Apple Tree

I scrambled down the marble stairs as I heard Abu at the front door. He brought with him the smell of fried samosas, freshly printed newspaper ink and *paan*. The bells on my new anklets jingled as I scurried.

"One day you will fall down those stairs and that pretty face won't be so pretty anymore," he scolded. The residue of the red paan peeked from the corners of his mouth. The paan stuck to his thick mustache. I chuckled. I placed my palm over my mouth.

"Now what is funny?" The words were muffled as he tilted his head up careful not to spit paan out of his mouth. Every morning Abu bought a fresh stack of paan leaves from our garden. Dadi prepared them for him in the morning. The leaf was neatly folded into a triangle with a filling of betel nut, tobacco, fennel seeds and an assortment of herbs. He chewed paan after his morning chai and didn't wash his mouth until the next morning before his chai.

I grabbed the newspaper out of his hand and ran. My white shimmery skirt dragged across the floor.

"I bought that for myself Zahida!" He yelled behind me.

I had already made it across a few rooms.

"Why do you even let her read that stuff? I never learned to read. She needs to focus on growing up. Look at her running away like a child and getting her new dress dirty. She's seventeen years old. Seventeen! Find some suitors and get her married!" Ami shouted to Abu.

"Oh, let her read Kurash. Zahida can read and get married. The English women do both nowadays," Abu teased.

"Then go. Be English, both you and your daughter. Ask the English women to make you rotis and korma," Ami mumbled under her breath and Abu chuckled.

It was a typical day in our household. Now Abu would spend the rest of the evening complimenting and winning her back just to see her angry eyebrows ease and her lips resist a smile.

I sat on the swing in the largest balcony of the mansion with the view of the garden.

Somewhere in the distance a priest played ancient melodies on a flute. The sweet sound was carried through the low hills of the dreamy city. The green hills were painted as far as I could see. Our rows of trees in the garden seemed miniature compared to the hills in the background.

I crinkled open the newspaper. The ink transferred onto my fingertips where henna should be on a young woman's hands. I read everything since I can read. It was a gift to be able to read and write. And an even rarer gift for women. Ami couldn't read. She could read Arabic like most Muslims, but she couldn't hear the voice of the writer through the words. Sometimes I read to her but she didn't have much interest in the world beyond Abu's, ours, and our home.

I flipped to the politics section of the *Dainik Bhaskar Paper.*

DISCUSSIONS ROAR AS MUSLIM LEAGUE PROPOSES THE IDEA OF PAKISTAN

The Muslim League Party propose Pakistan. Pakistan will be the nation for Muslims. India will be split into two with Muslims on one side and Hindus and Sikhs on the other. The Muslim League promises a better life for all the Muslims willing to donate and build Pakistan. It will be a true nation where Muslims will be treated as equal. The Muslim League plans to win the election.

Pakistan. What was that? Pak; the root of the word meant pure and clean. A greed grew in my heart as I read through the article. The word equal tasted like the residue of honey and warm milk on the tip of my tongue. Win; another word that had a similar taste but with a bitter aftertaste.

I wanted the Muslim League to win against the Congress. Winning seemed like an urgency. The thought struck me like a lightning bolt; right there and then in that moment Pakistan had been created in every heart in India.

This election divided us, whether the country was divided or not. The election pitted us against one another. I wanted to parade with the sweet taste of a win around the entire neighborhood as I did with having the largest and healthiest cow. The

Muslim League did win the election and I did experience the sweet taste of gloating. The bitter after taste however, was yet to come. *This was the last day I identified as an Indian.*

Chapter Five
A Bitter Victory

A bright light flashed outside my window in the middle of the night. As the world around me started to make sense I understood what it was--fire. Something or someone was being tormented in flames. It soared like an explosion. I stood there in the arched frame of the large window watching the flames.

My hair and midnight blue silk skirt blew as the fan above me spun at the rate of my heartbeat. I grabbed my ultramarine blue dupatta from my canopy bed and rushed downstairs. I froze on the last step; a habit I picked up from knowing my place as the child in the home.

Abu paced back and forth across the big

foyer. Ami had her head down and looked pale. *Was she sick again?*

"Don't tell the children about this. They better not find out. Keep them away from this. It will all die down and go away. I slipped Nadeem an extra bill when I went to the servant quarters. The fire will be put out and his lips are sealed," Abu's words came out in an informative tone like they did when he was discussing a business meeting.

"Like what? The Calcutta riots? Like how that went away? Away with four thousand people in their graves?" Ami replied.

I placed my palm over my mouth. Four thousand people died? Was what I saw, a person on fire? I glued myself to the wall and steadied my breathing to listen in.

"That fire was just the beginning of it. A signal. A message from those Hindus," Ami said. I heard her mutter protection prayers in Arabic under her breath. A silence lingered between them for a while. It made the air tense.

"We have to leave," Ami whispered. She said it like the last words of a book. Like after those words there was nothing else to do but to close the book and ponder, long and hard.

"Absolutely not! Are you out of your mind Kurash? I am not leaving everything that I built for this Pakistan. I built this. All of this without a father. I worked day and night to make this life for you and our family. I am not going to throw it away. You don't just throw that away. You don't just throw away your entire life like that." A web of veins appeared near the temples of Abu's forehead.

"Fine, don't," she replied but her mouth spilled more words as her own web of veins appeared.

"You never really supported the Muslims anyways. Why am I asking a man who barely sees the sight of a mosque to support the Muslims?"

I covered my mouth once again as if I had heard my own mother curse.

"I didn't mean that...Jaan," Ami whispered.

A heavy tired silence filled into the room and her eyes brimmed with tears.

"I am just a little scared. We have seven daughters. I don't want to leave them at the hands of these Hindus, they are disbelievers. They don't believe in God," Ami said.

"They are my friends Kurash Jaan. They have been my friends. They have loaned me money and helped me when I was a boy without a father. Ram is like a brother to me. I was a young boy who came to this city with nothing but an old mother and a baby brother. They believed in me. This is my home. This is our home. This is our place, forever. It will end here."

"I know." She took his hands in hers and pulled him close enough for me to turn away.

I didn't think it was possible what Ami was saying that we could just move. This was our home. There was no reason to move. Abu and Ram Kaka were like brothers. They loved each other. There were no sides.

It was one of the custard apple trees. It still stood strong like a tall dark tower. It hovered over the entire garden with no branches, no leaves and no custard apples.

"Should we cut it down?" Abu asked me.

"Who did this Abu?"

"What do you mean who did this? I told you, it caught fire from one of the lanterns." His eyes turned away and he collected the fallen branches. I helped him and together we cleaned up the mess in silence, not knowing that it was only the first of many innocent trees.

Later that evening, I decided to stroll out to the market. The sun was setting, and the city was lightening up. Small chai hotels turned on their strings of little colorful lights. The big Shiva temple stairs were lined up by *diyas*. The mosque across the street showcased its own set of lanterns. A green flag hovered high above one of its pillars. The flag was a dark green with a white crescent moon and star. It soared high above the city. Below on the mosque doors a big banner was posted. It read the following:

PAKISTAN ZINDABAD
THE MOSQUE IS COLLECTING DONATIONS IN THE BUILDING OF PAKISTAN

A band of supporters huddled around the entrance. I watched like an outsider in

The Custard Apple Tree

front of my own mosque. A tall woman with almond eyes and a large mole on her left cheek approached me. She matched the outfit of most Muslim women; a black *abaya* with a matching headscarf.

"Salam, Zahida beti I am so happy to see you. Your mother has told me a great deal about her eldest daughter."

"Your mother didn't tell you who I am? I am Bushra Begum. I recognized you by a photograph your mother showed me. I am with a group of Muslim League supporters, and we are marching from town to town collecting support for building Pakistan. It's a true fight for equality for all of our Muslim brothers and sisters to have rights and practice Islam. I am surprised your mother hasn't told you about me. She has been a real help handing out posters, talking to locals, and her great donation last week. With even a handful of supporters like your mother, Pakistan will be a reality."

I wanted to tell her how stupid she sounded. How God wasn't found in Pakistan. God could be found anywhere and everywhere she looked. Like the famous 14th century poet Hafiz said, *"The place where you are right now, God has circled on a map for you."*

"I am glad to hear that but just what did she donate?" I forced a smile that revealed my bottom crooked teeth.

"Like most of the women your mother gave gold," Bushra Begum said. "These beautiful gold anklets." She pulled out my anklets from her pockets. They sparkled in the night.

A fire stirred in my heart. *Those were mine!* Ami had no right giving them away.

"It was lovely chatting with you Zahida. *InshAllah* Pakistan will become a reality. Tell your mother I forward my Salam."

"Allah Hafiz," I watched as her black cloak disappeared into the sunken night of the Jabalpur alleys. I never saw her or my gold anklets again.

I had to get a copy of the Calcutta newspaper before the evening grew deeper. I walked to the local stand which sold newspapers, books and cheap poetry written by starving local artists.

The Custard Apple Tree

"Can I get the Calcutta paper Kabir Kaka?" I dropped a coin on a stack of novels. The old man glared at me with knitted eyebrows. The red dot between his eyebrows was a clear sign which side of the segregation he was on.

"We are not selling to Muslims," he cried out.

I had bought books from Kabir Kaka since I could read. Abu brought me here on Saturday evenings to pick out a stack for the next week. I stared at him. His once familiar eyes were now stone. I knew not to press the matter any further. Somehow the streets of the only home I knew seemed foreign. The cold swamped Jabalpur taking it into what would be one its harshest winters to come in history.

I found another book stall near the mosque with a Muslim vendor. I purchased a copy of the Calcutta newspaper. Lately no newspaper made its way inside our home.

That night the chai hotel was empty, apart from a few children who worked as the waiters playing in the corner. I slouched into the plastic chairs and ordered a cup. A young boy placed a small clear glass of steaming pink chai on the metal table. I dropped a set of coins. My mind played scenarios of Ami spotting me with a newspaper in my hand, one foot over my opposite knee taking loud slurps out of a small dirty cup. It was these little battles that I lived for. I knew that I couldn't do more as a girl, but these little moments were enough. I crinkled open the newspaper.

CALCUTTA RIOTS ARE ONLY THE BEGINNING OF THE VIOLENCE IN INDIA

Riots took the streets of Calcutta. This was only the start of what is being called by many reporters the week of long knives. The numbers are rounding up the 4,000 deaths and around 100,000 residents have been left homeless within the span of 72 hours. Neighbors have turned on each other to take direct action on the ongoing unresolved issue of forming Pakistan. The Muslims took to the streets with weapons as an act to show that they will no longer live in a country with Hindus. This has shifted from a political matter to a matter of the people.

The image of the burning tree flashed before my eyes, but as a burning person this time. That could have been any of us. The Muslims in Calcutta had lost it. This wasn't about winning anymore; this was a war on religion.

I reached for the chai glass, but it had gone cold. I gathered my belongings and made my way home. A home for how long, it seemed more and more uncertain.

⌣

The house didn't smell like fresh rotis and I didn't hear blaring laughter. I took off my dupatta as I stepped in. Ami, Abu and Dadi sat on the elaborate sofas imported from China with carvings of all sorts of dragons. Their eyes were glued on me. I stood awkwardly in the foyer. A minute passed, then another. The ticking of the large gold wall clock blared in the empty space.

"Salam," I coughed out the words.

"Zahida, we need to talk to you," Abu said.

I set my bag down. "Am I getting married?"

"No, it's not that. There is no marriage

right now. This is about you leaving."

"Leaving? I went on a walk." First my gold, now they want to take away my freedom as well.

"You can't go out like that anymore at all, not even on a walk." Abu rubbed his palms together.

"But I have always left the house. Why not now?" I wanted him to say it. I was tired of pretending everything was fine. Abu cleared his throat, but words didn't follow. The same tired silence filled our home once again. I knotted and unknotted the end of my dupatta over and over again until it started to wrinkle.

"I know what's happening. We are going to lose our home...I am not a child anymore." My tone was harsher than I intended. I saw a fire flash in Ami's eyes. She rushed towards me.

"Get up," she barked. I refused to get up. Ami yanked me up by my forearm.

"You are a child. How dare you speak to your father in that tone. How dare you leave the house. Know your place as a woman. Your place is in this home, now and forever," she spat.

"I...went...for...a...walk," the words came out between hiccups.

"Kurash let go of her arm," Abu demanded.

But a rage made Ami's judgment fuzzy.

"You..you are not even allowed to breathe without my permission." Ami clenched her teeth and dug her nails into my arm. I inhaled sharply, put my chin up and met her eyes. She forgot it was her blood that flowed through my veins, and I said:

"Brave, coming from a thief. I guess you are allowed to give away my gold anklets to a random lady for a cause that has divided us all, but the real crime here is my evening strolls."

She dropped my arm. As I saw her glass eyes melt, I realized what I had done. I had outed her.

Abu raged towards her. He didn't look my way. He pointed at the staircase with his eyes cemented at Ami and said:

"Zahida. Upstairs. Now."

"But Abu I can explain..." My words got lost as his blood shot eyes pierced my soul.

He pointed to the staircase once again and I went up the marble staircase. I watched them below.

Yelling replaced the evening laughter for the first time in our home.

"How dare you? You are going behind my back now. I am your husband. You didn't ask for my permission. Permission isn't the right word; you didn't even care to tell me that this is what you have been up to. All those late nights. Teas with the ladies, huh! It all makes sense now," Abu's voice thundered through the entire house.

"I don't need your permission for what I do with the gold I came into this marriage with. I can give them to whomever I please. I believe in this cause. A place for us Muslims, a pure place where our daughter will be safe, where our sons can have jobs. Real jobs in the government without having to work twice as hard. This is *Jihad*, and as a Muslim I have all permission from my God to give whatever I have; my money, my support and if it calls my body to fight."

I swear I saw Ami's eyes glimmer as she

talked about Pakistan.

"This is a fight for all those who don't have money like we do. This is a fight for my Muslims sisters and brothers who suffer everyday. So, yes, I will fight not for me, but for our coming generations. A land that will actually belong to them, where they won't be the lesser people; money or not," Ami bellowed.

Abu was stunned at her bitter tone. "I pray to God you never get to see this land that comes before your husband and your family. The land that comes before your daughter's future." He had a look of pure disgust on his face.

I spent the rest of that night wishing I was still a child. An oblivious, innocent child.

Chapter Six
Faith

Faith is one of the few virtues that makes a man both vulnerable and strong. It's power and absolute devoted helplessness all in one word. As the days passed, I saw faith not as a principle but as a wall that had grown between my parents.

Ami grew stubborn. A kind of stubbornness I had never seen before. Pakistan was her golden ticket to paradise and none of us came before it. She spent her days at the mosque. Abu spent his days in his study.

Now a green flag soared from the roof of our home as well. Groups of Muslim men danced and cheered as they passed through our narrow walkways. Women came to the house with news and every part of the city had been segregated.

It was one of these days I went to see Bhavna after my Quran lesson. The alleyway to her neighborhood was jammed with a rally of Congress supporters. The Hindus held posters of Gandhi. Cows decorated in bells and flowers trudged beside them. They screamed *Jai Hind* on the top of their lungs. I recognized some of the young men from Abu's gatherings; where the men and their sons would sit long after dinner smoking cigars and munching paan.

One of them particularly stood out; Aarav. He was a tall young man with prominent facial features, deep set dimples and forest green eyes. Our interaction was always limited but once he grabbed a glass of water from the kitchen while I was cleaning pots. I always wondered why he hadn't told a servant to fetch the glass. It was always something I wanted to ask him if we talked again.

That day I was sitting on the floor scrubbing large pots from dinner. The maids would have done it, but Ami made me do it every now and then in case my *naseeb* didn't have a husband who was rich husband. Aarav had been standing there for God knows how long. Two curls kept making their way to the front of my face and I kept using the back of my hand to push them away every thirty seconds. My face was flushed, and my pink dupatta draped over my shoulder. I always wore my dupatta over my head around men who weren't immediate family, but at that moment all my concentration was on the pots.

Aarav finally cleared his throat. I looked up, annoyed, thinking it was one of my brothers. When I saw Aarav, the blood rushed to my cheeks. As I rushed to get up, I knocked over a few pots. The metal banging rang both our ears. A thin stream of water and soap spilled down the marble floor. I wiped my hands on the end of my shirt and draped my dupatta loosely over my head.

"I am so sorry. I didn't mean to disturb you. Do you happen to have a glass of water?" He said in the softest voice I had ever heard from a young man.

The Custard Apple Tree

I heard Aarav sing at the Hindu festivals. A huge bonfire was lit in the city square where they staged a retelling of Hindu stories. Aarav sang balled after balled with praises to the Gods. I watched him immerse himself into the melody. He forgot everything around him and just sang.

I peered at him between crowds of people as the fire flamed to the sky behind him as he sang ancient hymns. The melody stirred something inside of me. The young man whose voice I waited to hear, stood in front of me scratching his head.

"Of course, there is water. This is a kitchen. That was stupid. Excuse me, I am usually a lot more intelligent and well-spoken than this," he stuttered.

I remained silent, didn't meet his gaze and dished him a steel glass of chilled water from the clay pot. He stood there taking small sips of the water.

"Wow this is some good water. It's really cold and really good." He took sips. "Did you make this water?" He asked.

A chuckle escaped my lips. He followed it

with a nervous one and just like that I worked up the courage to look into those green eyes. I had never seen such eyes. It was rare to have colored eyes in Jabalpur. They were the green of an emerald. I had seen the stone once on a bride. It was set into a bed of gold around her neck. His eyes glimmered under the lantern lights in the gloomy evening. It was as if God had put life into the stone. He was handing me back the glass and I hadn't realized. When I did, my shy gaze met the ground once again. Then I turned back toward my chores.

"Your hair looks pretty like that," he said and curled his lips into a childish smirk.

Ever since then whenever Ami braided my hair, I told her to leave out two of the front strands. Every time I saw him, a smile inevitably took over my face. He lingered around the front of our house talking to my father after the gatherings were long over with his hands in his pocket. He kept stealing glances at me as I cleaned already polished furniture.

Aarav volunteered to tutor Zahid and Majid and did any other task that could be done. I found him fixing old bulbs, returning borrowed books to my father, and even raking dried leaves. In the evenings I caught him roaming behind the house as I came onto the rooftop to collect dried laundry. The moon always hung over us. I admired the moon as he admired me. I thought about all the things I would say to him over and over again. I thought about what he would say back.

I saw him in the poetry I read. The green eyes merged with the words on the paper.

No Hindu came around our mansion anymore and I hadn't seen Aarav for months. I spent long nights waiting for him on the rooftop folding and refolding the same laundry. Ram Kaka was the only Hindu that came to our mansion. He visited after the sun had long set. The path through the garden was cleared of lanterns for him. Abu and Ram Kaka discussed each side. Last week he came with three red barrels. I overheard the conversation from Abu's study and watched them through the crack in the door.

"What is this Ram?" Abu's eyes gaped at the large barrels.

"It's protection."

"Protection from what?"

"Sit down Murad. Just sit for a minute," Ram Kaka said.

He didn't sit. Abu rubbed his palms together, waiting for the answer he didn't want to hear.

"I don't know how to explain this to you Murad. I don't. I don't want to. But those people out there, they are not your friends. The Hindus are not your friends. The Muslims are no longer my friends either. They have hatred in their hearts for you. I sit with them everyday. I work with them. Murad, I live with them, I am them. I hear the things they say. I am like your brother, but they are not. They see your daughters as Muslims. Just Muslims." Ram Kaka's brown eyes softened.

"Do you know what it means to be a Muslim where the Hindu is majority?" Ram Kaka asked. "It's like being a deer in a lion's den. You saw what the Muslims in Calcutta did to the Hindus. If I was living in a Muslim community, I would want you to give me these barrels Murad. They have all become animals, all of us and we have to learn how to survive."

Abu paced around the study.

"But what, what would I do with barrels of gasoline?" Abu knew the answer, but he hoped that Ram Kaka would say something else.

"They will never spare Kurash and your daughters."

I watched my six little sisters play in the room across with wooden dolls. From the room escaped a mix of laughter, screaming, crying and giggling. The sounds of childhood.

"They won't show mercy. Not even to Zubeida. What is she, two? Imagine what they would do to Zahida. She is seventeen. Murad, she is a young woman." He took Abu by the shoulders.

"Keep these barrels hidden. Okay? Just somewhere in the house. Tell the girls where they are. If something happens to you, Zahid or Abid. Burn them. The girls and Kurash," Ram Kaka informed.

Abu stumbled back. Books from his wooden desk scattered across the marble floor. Ram

Kaka went to pitch him some water. Instead of the water, Abu grabbed Ram Kaka's arm and they both sat down. Abu buried his head into Ram Kaka's shoulder and sobbed. He clenched his shirt with his fists and drenched it with tears; he wailed like a child.

"They are my daughters Ram. They are the *noor* of my eyes. How do I burn the light of my eyes?" Abu shrieked.

That night I saw Abu do something he had never done before. He laid out a prayer mat and prayed. Abu knelt his head down to the God he hadn't asked anything from in fifty years.

Not when he lost his father.

Not when he spent days without food.

And not when he slept on park benches with a mother and a little baby brother but that night he begged.

In the morning when I got out of bed for prayer, I found him with his forehead kneeled to the ground fast asleep. A pearly light poured through the white curtains in his study. The shelves with books from all over the world towered over him. I pulled him up and walked him to the green velvet couch. I took off my shawl and placed it on him. I brushed back his curls with my fingers and traced where horizontal lines formed on his forehead. I held his large hand in the small of mine and all I could manage to say was,

"Everything will be alright." He was sound asleep, but I repeated the words over and over again, knowing they needed to be heard more by my own ears than his. His warm hands lulled me into a deep sleep as well and a thought kept festering fear; *Abu wouldn't burn us. It couldn't come to that.*

I saw Aarav differently. He cheered on. He saw me as I was about to turn the corner. I stared into his emerald eyes. His lips didn't curl into a smile this time and mine didn't either. I didn't shy away. I stared and his eyes saddened. He stopped chanting. He had picked a side. We were all on a a side, but he had picked his. His eyes said a last goodbye and mine a much colder one.

Chapter Seven
Aarav

It was an anxious night. The kind of night where anxiety crawls into every crevasse and wrinkle of the sheets beneath you. It slitters underneath you, over you and flows through your veins. You toss and turn but sleep doesn't come, and the air stiffens your muscles.

Abu was gone away to Ahmedabad for work. He refused to give up work. He woke up everyday, had his morning chai followed by a paan and then arranged the day's meetings. He hid the barrels, ignored the flags, and continued living in denial. Bags formed underneath his eyes, a new line appeared with his tired smile each day, but he worked.

That's what he was good at and in the time of uncertainty he did what he could do best; survive in familiarity.

We were alone. I spent many and many nights without my father but tonight felt unsettling. The streets were quiet and occasional sounds of stray dogs howling and owls hooting disturbed the eerie silence. The marble floor felt cold and the spaces in the house hollow. Through the night I thought I heard wailing. I was unsure if they were my own or just the voices in my head. I tossed and turned. The day didn't seem to come, and the night didn't seem to pass. My chest tightened. I felt stuck.

Then suddenly violent banging came from our front door.

Ya Allah could it be time. Time for our last hour.

The large wall clock showed 3:34 AM. I got out of bed. The house was dark. Ami was lying on the sofa. A dull candle lit her pale face. She looked paler than usual. Her hair flowed down from the sofa to the floor. Her body caved into the sofa's cushion surface.

She looked weary. The knocking on the door remained steady.

Bang. Bang. Bang.

"Ami, who is it?" I approached her but I quickly realized that Ami had left us. Nothing mattered to her anymore. Meals weren't served on time, prayers weren't muttered on us in the morning, and she didn't wear jasmine flowers in her hair. The flowers sat on her vanity every morning. They turned a pale yellow throughout the day. In the morning Abu threw them out and replaced them with fresh ones. But they never made their way into her braid.

"It's them, the disbelievers. This is the end. It's over Zahida. This is what they are doing. They are going house to house killing Muslims." Her voice was calm. As if she was ready, as if she had been ready for death but the rest of us weren't ready.

Bang. Bang. BANG.

Either the door would burst open or my heart. Ami drifted into a sleep. I tried to shake her out of it, but sleep pulled Ami away. My hands shook violently, but I had to do something. I recited God's name under my breath.

BANG. BANG. BANG.

The knocking fell into a rhythm of threes. It got louder with each knock. I searched the house for anything that could protect me. I ran over to Abu's study where he kept a collection of fancy hockey sticks from winning games in a showcase. I scrambled to find the keys and grabbed a hockey stick. I had to do something. I had to.

"Who...is...it?"

My heart raced, my stomach did cartwheels, and I thought I was going to face the angel of death. My sweaty fingers clenched the wooden stick so tight that my fingers turned red. No one answered but the banging stopped. A small whisper came from the other side of the door.

"It's Aarav."

I stayed silent.

"Zahida open the door. It's Aarav."

I remained silent. Thoughts whirled in my head.

"Your Aarav," he whispered.

The words softened my heart. I threw aside the hockey stick, unlatched the locks and wedged open the door. I lunged towards Aarav when my eyes met his green ones. I wrapped my arms around him, and tears stung my eyes. My entire body shook against his steady body.

"They are coming," he said.

"Who?" I knew the answer. I cupped his worried face with my hands.

"They know your father isn't home and they plan to..." The words got lost and his eyes lost to mine.

"They plan to do what?"

"It's some drunken guys. They are going around raping girls and destroying some of the communities' Muslim homes. They know that your father isn't home Zahida."

The words didn't process. He spoke fast. A pit in my chest grew the size of a cannon ball. A moon hung low in the sky. I looked into his eyes. They melted and softened at the touch of my fingers. My eyes welled up again and this time his did too. The gold coin necklace around his neck glowed under the light of the lantern. "Come with me," he said.

"I'll come with you," I responded. "That sounds okay, it sounds better than here." My soft skin burned as I rubbed the tears and took a deep breath.

"Let me get Ami and everyone else." I turned to rush inside but Aarav grabbed my wrist.

"I have my own family Zahida. I mean you. You come with me."

"Just me?"

"I can't save you all. But I can save you. I have to save you."

I peered back into the dark living room where my old pale mother slept.

"We can start over again. You can become a Hindu. We can take the train to Mumbai. You can teach. I can sing and work. We can start a life far, far, far away from this. This mess."

I pulled my hand away from his. I stepped back and realized my dupatta wasn't on my head.

"I am a Muslim."

"Well, this is what you Muslims have done.

You greedy, dirty Muslims think you deserve a country of your own."

The words stung because I knew they were true. We were the lesser people in India and always had been. I knew my place in society when I didn't argue against the Hindus going ahead in lines at cinemas, banks and hospitals.

"Leave." I crossed my arms.

"What?"

"Leave my house. My father isn't home." He grabbed my arm. This time his force was strong.

"You are coming with me."

"Let go of my arm."

"I love you Zahida. I have loved you for years." From the far end of the street a band of men marched with torches.

"But you don't love my people..."

The hollering of the men became louder.

"Aarav, I see them. The men. Let go of my arm. I need to go inside. I need to hide. I need to hide Ami and Banu and Majid and Abid."

"You have to come with me!" Aarav yelled. "I can save you."

"I don't need you to save me. I have my

God and I have my people." I struggled to get my arm out of his hand. The wind roared and my long black curls blew with it.

"You are coming with me. I didn't wait years and years for this to be our ending. I sacrificed your family to have you." And the emeralds looked lifeless once again. And I knew. Aarav sent those men. He wanted me at any cost.

A lightning bolt lit up the sky and silver blades of rain cascaded down. The droplets drenched us. We stood there soaked in the rain as the sky photographed the moment with one bolt after another. He let go of my arm. He had lost me, and I had lost him. I saw the men turn onto the corner of our alleyway.

"There was no other way, Zahida. Your father would have never approved of me."

"And now I don't approve of you."

I shut the metal doors. I sat with my back against the door dripping like a wet dog; aching and wailing. On the other side of the door, I heard the laughs of the drunken men. They hooted about how seven young girls lived here for them to borrow in the cold night. Aarav fought them. He screamed like a mad man.

"You will not hurt her. You hear me? You will not!" Aarav's voice boomed.

I heard him drop to his knees. It took all of my body's strength to not unlatch the door. I saw Ami in the hazy light of the candle, and I stuffed my mouth with the end of my dupatta and let out silent screeches.

"Hear that. He's protecting a Muslim. He is one of them," a man growled.

I heard what sounded like the end of a knife plunge into someone. As the metal met flesh, Aarav let out a scream. It was a scream that could have raised the dead. The angel of death did visit our doorstep that night. It was the last time I heard Aarav's sweet voice.

My mind never played his voice singing melodies again; it was always that scream. Aarav lay on the other side of that door as the pebbles of rain met with his blood and beat the earth. *That door.* That door was faith that wedged between my parents and now me and Aarav. The men left.

They were drunk and had had their fun.

I didn't open the door. I was frozen. I was frozen there all night as the blood of the man I loved cascaded down our marble stairs. I was helpless, or had I picked a side after all?

I was in my bed when I woke up the next day. I stared at the ceiling until the room came back to me. Until all the little pieces finally started to come back to me. The chandelier, the morning light hitting its reflective glass, my skin which felt heavy with layers of tears, the endless tangles in my curls, the shooting pain in the left side of my head, and Aarav.

The stairs were washed and there was no trace of Aarav's body. I found Abu setting the table with new plates. They were a fine white with gold trims.

"Oh Zahida, good you're awake. Look at these plates I got from Ahmedabad, aren't they just beautiful? I was thinking the gold was a little too much but then the Kapoor's told me it was real gold and I had to purchase them."

I stared at his eyes blankly.

"Abu, I can't do this anymore."

I slammed my fist into the table.

He continued to clean the plates with a tablecloth.

"I can't do this anymore. Last night. Do you even know what happened last night? A man. A man died-." I choked.

He kept polishing the plates.

"Abu. Abu," I whined.

"Why are you dressed like that?" He asked.

"What?"

"Why haven't you changed for the day? You slept in that outfit, right?"

"What?"

"Did you or did you not sleep in that outfit last night?" He asked.

"Yes, I did."

"Then go upstairs and change."

I stared at him in disbelief. He held the plate up to his nose and wiped the same spot. I wasn't there, or he wasn't there, it didn't make a difference anyways.

Every night after that the screams of Aarav tormented me.

Chapter Eight
Monsoon

I used to wonder how people just recovered from tragedies like the funerals of their parents and spouses. I learned that those people had battled so many griefs in their life that sadness was familiar to them. It was no longer something they feared. Sadness is an emotion that we would dwell in for most of our adult lives. That's why they say that childhood is so precious because it was untouched by the sorrows of life. We dwell in this sadness so deep that it becomes us, it becomes life, and eventually it feels safe.

The days pressed on and chatter grew. Ami spent all her long days and even longer nights preparing for our journey. She had bundles of stuff wrapped in luggages. She prepared all sorts of pickles, dried meats, and papad. She placed the items in the corner of the balcony living room which was drenched with forest green vines, colorful Rajasthani cushions and low wooden sofas. Abu never acknowledged the stuff and she never asked him to.

I saw the stuff pile on more and more everyday. Something new was always added; a small box of ancient China spoons, or exotic valuable silks. All of it seemed to perfectly fit in our home. It all had its own place. The fabrics had the closets and the chinaware had cupboards. But what was all that stuff without a home; it was old junk. Many of the Muslim families held yard sales. They lined up all their goods and sold it at rates which were so low they were basically free. They said that even a little bit of money was going a long way in Pakistan.

At the end of the night most of the stuff was left outside as bands of beggars scavenged through it. Beggars took over the once chirpy streets of Jabalpur. I had read an article about it becoming a hot business; to take the residence of the homes abandoned by Muslims in the bigger cities. Everywhere you looked a woman wearing a sari made up of rags with a newborn clung to her chest took charge of the streets. I scrunched my nose. I didn't like the poor. Ami always told me that they didn't choose to be poor, but they could work hard. They brought this poverty upon themselves.

As I passed them on the streets I lifted my chin and covered my nose with the end of my dupatta scoffing at their misery. They were found sleeping in the back of *rickshaws* at night. The city grew unsafe. It was like a door was being closed in on us. With everything in us we tried to hold on to Jabalpur. But Jabalpur like the rest of India had changed and there was no place in the new for the old. We all knew our place was somewhere else. Our place was in Pakistan.

It was a hot August day. It disturbed the long rainy monsoon days. It rained for weeks straight, day and night. Black umbrellas crowded the streets. A day like this was rare and cherished. The sun engulfed the city and it felt like the first normal day in months. Children paraded the streets with kites, a crowd of young Muslim and Hindu men lounged on the plastic chairs at the chai hotel and vendors sold spicy fritters with tamarind chutney. The warm day evoked something in everyone.

Abu planned a spontaneous picnic for us. We were all going to the Dhaundhar Waterfalls. The maids packed baskets of fruit, roasted cuts of meat and bottles of fresh guava juice. I saw Ami plant jasmine flowers in her hair that morning. The horse carriage rocked us left then right. I watched the city fade as we pulled away from it. My home got smaller, the mosque looked like an icon from a map and the people even smaller. It was slipping away; my home, my city and everything I had ever known.

Ami and Abu held hands. I wondered what got them to finally see each other. I wondered what it was about love that made you see only one another even when the entire world was moving and changing around you. I watched them. I savoured this happiness. They sat in the front of the carriage. Ami rested her head on Abu's shoulder.

Ami's skin was pasty. The sun made her appear paler. Her hair had become frayed at the ends, now only a thin braid dangled out of her jasmine crown. Ami's sari blouse was loose. As a little girl I pinched her exposed back as she did chores. She got so mad, and I ran away giggling. But now in place of that fat was a bony rib cage.

Ami seemed small against my father. She was never one to seem small against a man. She stood with him; tall and firm. Now she slouched bent inward into a slight C shape. I watched as Abu took both her hands into his and blew warm air into them. It was a hot day, even my cotton shalwar kameez itched.

The falls finally arrived. We sat with the view of the cascading water, it misted on our faces. I watched as my younger siblings ran around in circles. Kites soared in the sky and the wind carried the smell of freshly fried samosas. I read for most of the day. I read

The Custard Apple Tree

more of Rumi's poetry. I missed reading.

This time I didn't see Aarav's green eyes in the poetry.

This time I didn't hear his screams.

This time I didn't see the green flag.

All I saw was Ami and Abu's hands locked through every word I read. And there it hit me; it wasn't the house, the city, the books or the garden. It was my parents. If they were happy, if they found a way to stay together. I would be okay; I wouldn't lose anything. It would still be home.

As soon as we got home the sun left, and sheets of rain poured over the city like a curse. We were back. We were all back in that place. I dreaded this home. I almost wanted to leave. The night drew on and we settled near the fireplace. Dadi retired to bed early and was already asleep. The pebbles of rain and wind shook our doors and windows.

Most of the little ones had fallen asleep on the floor which was scattered with cushions and blankets. Zubeida's small fists bunched up my shawl as I stroked her dark hair. For a three-year-old she was small. She could fit into anyone's lap even Banu's who was only five. Zubeida curled in my lap like a small kitten with each part of her neatly tucked into herself.

A chill passed through the room all of a sudden. I brought my wool blanket up to my neck. Ami and Abu sat on the sofa. Ami wrapped herself in her shawl. I adored that shawl; a beautiful brown embroidered with fine red threads into flowers. She wore it from the monsoon season up until the last day of spring. The orange fiery light exaggerated her almond eyes; she looked peaceful and warm. Abu held onto her hand. Only then did I realize how tired they both were from being away from each other.

Abu asked me to read out of the book that had been glued to my hands all day. I cleared my throat and read with the most poise Urdu accent, "Goodbyes are only for those who love with their eyes because for those who love with their heart and soul there is no such thing as separation…death had nothing to do with going away. The sun sets. The moon sets.

But they are not gone. Written by the one and only *ustad* of poetry, Rumi."

I tilted my head to take a silly bow. Ami clapped as if it was the greatest thing she had ever heard. She never liked when I read. But her eyes welled up and for a moment I thought she might have actually been proud of me.

The clapping tired Ami, sending her into a cough attack; she shook violently. Then it hit me. Ami wasn't just pale or tired, she was sick. This whole time Ami was getting more and more ill, and we had ignored it. Now the only sounds that filled the room was the crackling of the fire and her heavy breaths. Abu got up but she tugged on his sleeve to keep him beside her.

"Let's go take you to the hakeem," he said. "This coughing is too much."

"In this weather? It's storming," her words took a strain on her.

"Ami, we have to try. You're unwell," I insisted.

"It's no use Zahida...I...won't make it." She was turning almost blue and beads of sweat pounced down her forehead.

"I don't care. We are going to get you to the hakeem," Abu replied. He rushed towards the front door and unlatched it. The door blew in gusts of cold wind and rain. It was no use. Abu knew it. He closed the door.

"Just sit beside me, please. I will be okay.... The storm will die down and then...we can go," she insisted. He sat down by her feet beside me on the floor.

"You're going to be fine Kurash Jaan. I have to take you to your beloved Pakistan, right? Who will take this crazy lady? Tell her Zahida."

Ami's eyes glimmered and her lips curled up into a smile. But tears replaced the happiness. She cried and cried. Ami cried and the sky cried. I froze like I did that night. I sat there in my frozen body with no words, no tears, and no thoughts. It was like I was watching a picture at the cinema or dreaming, and this wasn't really happening.

"I won't...make...the...journey. I won't even make...it...through....the...night." The words were held on by air. But they were words.

The Custard Apple Tree

The most real words I had heard from Ami's mouth in months.

"Don't say that. Kurash you are...my life. You are my dawn, my evenings, and my nights. You are my bringer of good days. I am nothing without you Kurash Jaan. Who will I tease when I come home? Who will I come home to?" He swallowed the pit in his throat. Her dimples painted the sweetest and saddest smile.

"Don't say that again Kurash Jaan. Hey, look at me. Look at them. All those little humans sleeping on the floor they need you. I need you. We all need to go to Pakistan. Make a house there and buy you the prettiest garden in the whole entire country." He shook her shoulders.

"I won't make it Murad. You and Zahida, you have to take all of them...and go. You have to do what's right...You have to go to Pakistan, Murad," her words got softer and softer.

Ami drifted and her eyes lost focus. Abu held her hands tight. I imagined it pained Ami. But she didn't look in pain, she looked still like the a steady river. Her breathing became less steady. The rain poured outside. The orange light fell on her face perfectly; she glowed. A curl rested on her cheek and her eyes, her eyes looked like they had the light of heaven itself in them. Even her tears became pearly droplets that shimmered on her perfect skin.

"I'll start praying. Everyday, five times a day. I'll talk to every Muslim. I'll sell the house and find us a way to get there. Anything, I will do anything, love. I'll stop leaving my shoes in the foyer. I'll stop buying and wasting money on gifts. I will place the world at your feet. I swear to God anything." Abu's words got knotted between the tears.

In that moment I swear as Abu was begging Ami to stay with him, I saw him; the angel of death. In the corner of the room a black shadow stood tall, like the burned remains of the custard apple tree.

"I want...you to take them to my Pakistan." Her words were barely whispers.

"I will. I will take them. I will take you. We will all go. Let's go right now." He got up and rushed towards the pile of things. Ami didn't let him though.

"Hold her," I said.

"What?" Abu asked.

"Hold her as she leaves us. Hold her Abu, she's going to her heaven."

Ami brought my chin up to her face.

"Zahida, be a good woman for a good man. And be a strong woman against a bad man... and read because a life worth dying for is one spent fighting for what you love, even if the whole world thinks you're a lost cause.... Be a woman who reads and writes better than any man."

A tear trickled down my cheek. Ami did live a life of purpose. Her life was entwined with ours and generations to come forever. It was because of Ami and women like her that a whole new nation was born.

Abu held her. I melted my head down on her lap. Abu let out small cries. His tears soaked her hair. I held her hands until the last of life left them.

"Murad take them to Pakistan. It's safe there. In the end you will see...there is only one God and Muhammad is his messenger." The fire blew out and with it the figure in the corner of the room also disappeared. Abu and I stayed there all night. When the rain stopped, and the sun finally rose, and the soft light of dawn finally seeped into our home Abu said,

"It's my fault. I wished that night that God never let her see the land that came before her husband."

Chapter Nine
A Bed of Jasmine Flowers

After that everything happened very fast and remains a blur in my mind. Abu spent every waking moment making Pakistan become our reality. Most of the Muslims in our city had already left. Abu worried that he would have to marry his seven daughters to Hindus; that too if they wanted us. A wild cough kept him awake at night as he chewed one paan after another. He spent the nights buried in books figuring out maps, roadways, and the entire geography of Pakistan. Jabalpur was in the middle of India. We were 1,077 kilometers away from Pakistan's border. The flights were all sold out and the borders were closing in a few days. But Abu refused to take the trains and buses loaded with strangers.

He didn't place jasmine flowers on their vanity anymore, instead they went in our garden where Ami lay at rest beside the two other graves. I watched him pray over the grave in the early morning and late evenings. Some nights when I looked outside from behind the curtain of my window, I saw Abu in the garden. He sat and wept. He never let the jasmine flowers that blanketed Ami's grave dull. Her grave glowed like a bed of snow in the green luscious garden. Even at night it was illuminated. The burnt custard apple tree towered over them. Tall, dark and strong. Their love was nothing against the evil which infected every Indian's heart.

I didn't have time to miss my mother. My days were occupied by filling her shoes. I never realized how much she did until she was gone. Running a whole household wasn't a task fit for a seventeen-year-old. I felt small, lost and drowned in womanhood. I spent the day organizing duties to all the servants and maids, bathing and feeding my siblings and preparing for the unspoken journey.

Abu and I didn't speak much. Dinners were cut short because he attended to potential buyers of the home or because none of us felt hungry. Abu and I sometimes caught each other's glances as I hung chilis to dry and he gave a tour of the house. It was only for a moment. A quick look at each other. It would have been too much if we talked. It would have been too real. It was better to stay silent, to stay busy and to keep moving.

Our courtyard turned into a marketplace. All sorts of antiques, valuables and treasures were sold for a handful of rupees. Everything was to be sold.

Books. The books were what I grieved the most. I watched as my father's study was emptied shelf after shelf. I saw them part with me in the hands of strangers. Each book held the memories of Abu's strong reading voice lulling me into my dreamy childhood. Now the words slipped through my own two hands and there was nothing I could do about it. We couldn't take the books. We couldn't take anything really. We couldn't even take our mother. She would be left here on this land, alone. Something inside me told me that I would be the last of my family to ever see this land again. I soaked in the sweet air, sauntered barefoot in the garden every chance I got, ate as many custard apples as I could, and mopped the beautiful marble floors over and over again. I spent the nights in the balcony watching the stars above. I wanted to hold it; in my eyes, in my touch and remember this home forever. I loved this home more than any home I ever lived in again.

Dadi sat out on the balcony all day. She didn't speak much either. She didn't make warm *halwa* or hide us behind her fat belly when Abu scolded us. My grandmother was the heart of the family. She was the whispers and prayers that made us stronger.

One evening as we all sat around the table in silence picking at our plates of roasted lamb and naan, Dadi broke her silence.

"I don't want to go," she said.

"Dinners over everyone. Go upstairs," Abu said and wiped the corners of his lips with a napkin. My siblings had learned the hard way to stay out of his way these days, they all picked up their plates, placed them in the kitchen and headed upstairs.

"You too Zahida."

"You don't get to do that," I said.

"You're a child. I want you away from all this."

"I am in this. In fact, I am this."

"Don't argue. Go on upstairs."

I felt myself grow, almost physically. The child that would have stopped in her tracks when she heard her elders argue was now grown.

"I watched a man die on those steps when you left us alone. I saw Ami and you fight. I saw her get sicker day by day. I buried my own mother. I am watching every part of my life slip away everyday bit by bit. So, excuse me Abu if I think I can handle a conversation between you and Dadi because that is what it would have taken. One conversation between you and Ami and maybe just maybe…"

My mind felt like it was on fire. It blazed from one thought to another. I was tired and I needed someone to blame. I needed to paint a villain to this story of unfortunate events, and I did the worst.

"And maybe just maybe Ami would have still been alive."

He already believed it was his fault and now I confirmed it. Even Dadi was taken back. Tears rushed to Abu's eyes, but I felt nothing but anger. We hadn't grieved. That's what happens when you don't grieve; sadness turns bitter. And you take that bitterness and carry it with you everywhere.

I was bitter. I was bitter and sad.

Abu cleared his throat and spoke to Dadi.

"You don't want to come?"

"I don't want to leave," she replied.

"Fair enough then you don't have to come. The children and I will leave soon. I will leave you the home. What happens to you after we leave is not my responsibility. You can stay if that's what you want." He dropped the napkin on his plate and left.

Dadi peered at me.

"Kurash raised you better than this Zahida," she said and left the table.

For the rest of the night Abu locked himself in his study.

It was the last hours before dawn. I couldn't sleep, Abu couldn't sleep either. Sleep was rare those days. I peered at him as he sat by the grave picking through each and every dull jasmine flower replacing it with new fresh ones. He spent hours replacing them all. A cold wind swept them off her grave. But he kept fighting the wind and putting them back on her grave. He struggled back and forth with the strong breeze. The wind won and Abu buried his tired face into his knees and wept.

I went out there. I sat beside him on the grass and put my hand on his shoulder. He took my shoulder and dug his face into it. I held him. His thin weary body melted into my muscles.

"I miss her just as much," my lips quivered. We sobbed until there were no more tears left.

The Partition of India in 1947

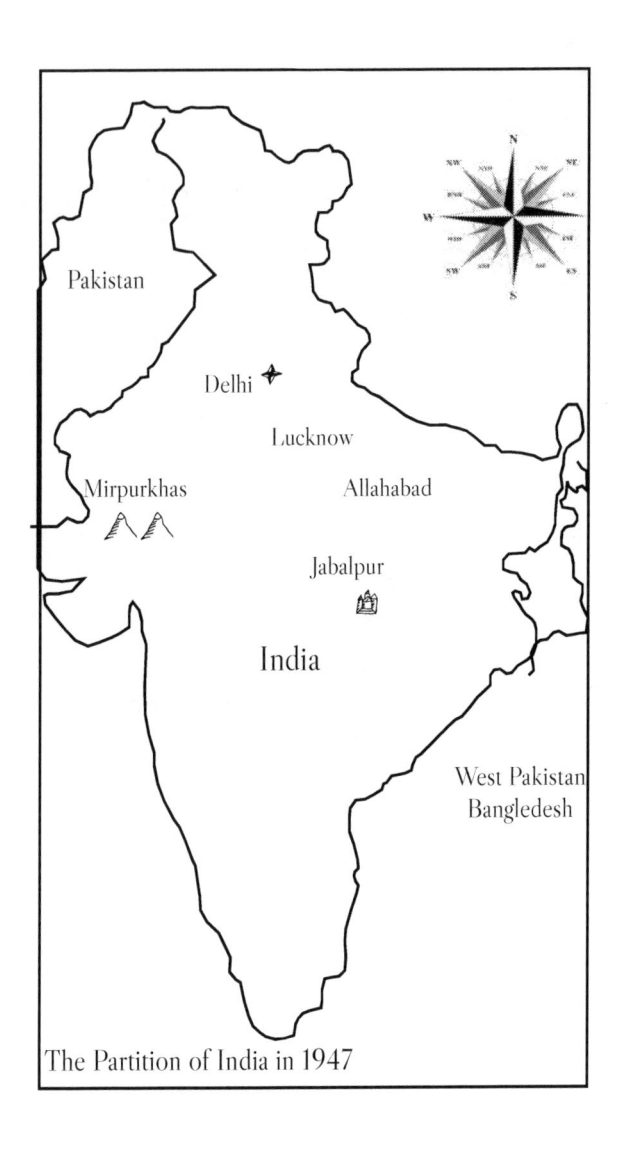

Chapter Ten
The Journey

That night felt surreal. When Abu came to my room, I was praying the night prayer on a Moroccan rug. I couldn't break out of my prayer. From the corner of my eyes, I saw that he had an open gash on his forehead which went from his scalp down to his right eyebrow. He held a rag drenched in blood over his wound. This could be the last prayer of my life. I knelt my head to the ground and pleaded to my God to protect my family and I on this unknown journey.

"We have to go! Now!" He shouted.

I finished my prayer by sending peace to both the angels that rested on my shoulders. As soon as I was done Abu vanished out of

The Custard Apple Tree

my door. My bed was not made. I glanced back at it; the floral sheets had thousands of wrinkles, the pillow was still pressed down in the middle, and the velvet green blanket draped down to the floor. The white flowy curtains cascaded down the canopy. It was a bed fit for a princess. I wondered what type of life waited for me in Pakistan.

I gathered my siblings in the foyer. I grabbed Ami's shawl from her room. I laid it out flat onto the bed. I placed her Quran, my gold bangles and handfuls of money on her shawl. I dug through her closet throwing fabrics left and right. I finally found it. It was a red lace dupatta I had seen Ami wear to gatherings since I was young. I always wanted it. I put the dupatta onto the shawl and tied both ends of the shawl making a small sack. Nothing else left the house except two bundles of preserved food that Zahid and Majid carried.

The house became a ghost house that night with its; unmade beds, half empty cups of chai, dirty plates left in the sink, clothes hung to dry, and a single light left on in one of the bedrooms on the fifth story. As we walked away from our home forever, I watched that one window which was the sole light against the dark tall mansion.

We left like thieves.

Abu set one last jasmine flower on Ami's grave. He took the dirt from her grave and filled it in his pockets. He kissed his palms and set them on her grave. "My Kurash. My jasmine flower, forgive me."

I ran into the garden and picked my very last custard apple.

We all sat on the donkey cart. Zubeida was on my lap and Banu snuggled underneath my arm. Dadi nestled the rest of them, and Abu sat beside the boys. The night was still. The house started to slowly drift out of sight. I didn't blink, not even once. I didn't want to leave. Ami's snow-white grave and that one room glowed as we grew farther and farther away from the mansion. Then those too became invisible and only the tall burnt tree towered over the property. The road got narrowed. As the donkey cart turned the corner to the main street, my home disappeared forever.

Train One

From Jabalpur
to Allahabad
Duration: 13 Hours

It was the last train out of Jabalpur leaving for the city of Allahabad. The city was founded by the Mughal King, Akbar. It was another Muslim city with rich Islamic history that would remain on the Indian side. This first train was just the beginning of a long route that would take us to the distant land that was already ours.

Dawn creeped onto the Jabalpur Junction Railway Station. Ram Kaka waited for us on a bench. I spotted him amidst the tsunami of people that flooded the station. He appeared to be the only Hindu with his vibrant red *kurta* and straight legged white pajama. His silver hair was parted neatly to the side, but he looked withered.

Abu knew him since the timeline of his better life began. It started with Ram Kaka beside him, and it would have ended with him beside him if it weren't for that night. He was his first friend when he came to Jabalpur alone. Abu never talked about his father; to this day it remains a mystery if his father had died or just left. All we knew was that he was gone; no headstone, no memories, and no stories. The young streets weren't kind to the Muslim boy, his baby brother and old mother.

Ram Kaka helped Abu get his first job at the age of ten as a shoe shiner. They spent hot days in the sun polishing the dirt off of British shoes. That's where they picked up their knowledge about politics, business, and the arts. Abu said that his talent was being the invisible dark skin boy at the feet of white men who had the whole world in their fists. He spent the evenings after earning the day's wage buried in books with Ram Kaka; who taught him everything he learned in school. And they grew up together in the dirty streets of Jabalpur.

Abu's brother lived in Delhi. Abu set his brother up with a business. Their family booked plane tickets to the city of Karachi in Pakistan at the start of the partition.

Ram Kaka rushed towards us from across the platform.

"Here." Ram Kaka placed something small in Abu's palm and closed it. They shared a simple nod followed by a firm brotherly hug. Words again became scarce. "You stay safe,

The Custard Apple Tree

Murad. Write me letters. Come visit if you get the chance. Maybe I can come visit you in Pakistan."

"InshAllah," Abu replied.

That was all. They couldn't say anything more. Ram Kaka touched Dadi's feet after that and she placed her hand on his head--a Hindu gesture to show respect to elders.

"Thank you for everything you did for my son," Dadi said with misty wrinkled eyes.

"Thank you for giving me the brother I never had."

Ram Kaka moved on to me. I touched his feet embracing our mixed cultures one last time. Then he lifted Zubeida into his arms and poked her nose. Her giggles made everything sadder.

"I'll miss you so much Ram Kaka....you think we will ever come back? Do you think we can ever come back home?" I uttered.

He continued to play with Zubeida.

"Of course. This is just temporary. They will realize that we all can't live without each other. That all Hindus and Muslims are Indians, it's been like that since the beginning of time. We are all different but one."

"Really?" A spur of hope tingled in my heart. Maybe this was just a vacation and we would be back home, and I could make the beds and turn off that one light.

"Like your Abu said if God wills."

Abu said one last goodbye to his friend as we boarded the train. There wasn't one inch of space; bodies were trampled onto one another to fit. A stale air which smelled of piss, sweat, and a stench of rotting corpses aroused from every corner. There was no place to sit, no place to stand, you just had to find a way to fit.

The engine turned on and the big machine screeched riding away from the platform. In the distance I saw Ram Kaka standing alone in the empty station as a hazy dawn creeped over the city. I saw the green hills of Jabalpur eventually turn into flat land.

I never saw my home, city or land again.

The stench of the train made me hurl every hour. There was a boy on the far end of the train. He was around the age of eight or ten.

The Custard Apple Tree

The rotting stench was coming from him. He wasn't with anyone. He leaned against the door with his eyes closed. His body had turned a grayish blue. His purple feet poked out of his pistachio green shalwar.

He was dead.

He was unclaimed and no one did anything about it. People kept moving. I watched him as the train rode from dawn to sunset and then to a dark sky splattered with stars above us.

"Abu."

He had finally fallen asleep.

"Yes," he mumbled out of a baffled sleep.

"I think that boy over there is dead."

"What boy, Zahida? There is no boy there?" I pointed at the child. Abu shook his head.

"There is no one there Zahida." I could still see him. I asked Zahid after.

"Zahid that boy there? Do you see him, he's dead?" Zahid shook his head as well. He saw nothing as the train swayed left and right. No one could see him. I still wonder to this day if that little boy was there or not.

As we got off that first train a bed of

maggots made a home on his body.

Still, no one touched him or tossed him, or saw him so he just rode on.

Until when? I wouldn't know.

Train Two

From Allahabad
to Lucknow
Duration: 9 Hours

The second train was straining on Dadi. She ran high fevers that didn't break. I spent the first few hours wetting the end of my dupatta in cold water and placing it on her forehead. Nothing cooled her down and the loud cheering of the Muslim League supporters didn't help either.

"Pakistan Zindabad!"

"We are on our way to heaven, people. You will earn double of what you earn here amongst these Hindus. They treat us worse than they treat their cows. Schooling will be free for all children. There will be new jobs for every able man. There will be no segregation or class difference. I promise you all Pakistan is our heaven in this world. Our Quaid-e-Azam Muhammad Ali Jinnah promised us. He promises us all a better life. There will be hospitals, women will not be raped, and peace will prevail. Say it with me everyone, Pakistan Zindabad!" The crowd roared with them. The words sounded rewarding.

Steel plates often went around with bland pickled onions and a watery lentil soup. After eating the food and licking every last grain

The Custard Apple Tree

with my fingers, I saw my reflection staring back. I looked worse than I smelled; my curls were tangled; I had a layer of dirt on my fair skin and my almond eyes resembled those of langur monkeys. A lady scrunched up her nose up at my stench. After two days of traveling this train finally rocked me into a deep exhausted sleep. It must have been four in the morning when the same man giving speeches started yelling,

"Fire, fire, fire!"

The most putrid stench sank through the entire train. Flames consumed the train parallel to us. It was like the tree outside my window that night. I covered Zubeida's ears as we heard the screams from the depths of hell. A child's hand gripped the metal railing of the window. The small hand didn't lead to a visible body. It was the sight of hell itself; red torchy flames and the screams of innocent people. From our train together we all recited the prayer for the deceased.

"Indeed, we belong to Allah, and to him we will return."

A Hindu mob appeared with swords and

torches from out of the smoke. That night thousands of men, women and children were burned to death. Our train started to move seconds after. The little hand in the train was still moving when I last saw it. The little fingers gripped around the metal bars wiggled in torment. I could do nothing but look away

Two days ago, Abu would have ripped apart a person who even spoke with a disrespectful tone and there he sat with his head dropped. Had we all changed that fast? There were no more speeches after that, no more cheering and no more hope. We all just wanted to make it to Pakistan, *alive.*

Train Three

From Lucknow
to Delhi
Duration: 13 Hours

My back muscles burned, I had developed blisters on my heels and the back of my throat was dry when we finally arrived at the Lucknow Charbagh Railway Station. All of that pain melted when I saw the architecture of the station. It was the most interesting building I had ever seen. It was a fusion between Islamic architecture and the colors of Rajasthan; rustic sandy reds with a neat pattern of white strokes. It went up in levels and the pillared domes got bigger and bigger. It was dressed in green and blue lights to liven up the night. Abu explained how it was another monument made by a Muslim architect in 1914.

A band of men dressed in black wearing belled anklets and eyeliner sat at the end of the platform singing *qawwali* - a form of Sufi Islamic devotional singing. They sang praises to the almighty and played the harmonium.

"*Rangreza O Rangreza*--the one who paints color, *Kyun faya Kyun*--referring to the Quranic verses be, and it is."

A group of little children gathered around the men, playing and singing. I urged my own

The Custard Apple Tree

siblings to go play. They all got up and ran in circles with the other children making little boats out of old newspapers. For a moment I thought maybe Pakistan won't be so bad. Abu acquired a great knowledge about Pakistan in the past weeks. He kept a small journal with notes and details of the land's layout. I was astonished to learn all that he knew.

"This is the city called Karachi, the capital. Our city in Southern Pakistan. In the region of Sindh; a vast desert. This ocean right here is the golden secret to making this the hub of the entire country. It will give us trade and access to a world of import and export. And look here." He pointed to the Indian side.

"They kept the most fertile lands of Punjab for themselves, but with the Northern heavens of Pakistan we can create the world's best tourism industry. I saw pictures of it Zahida. It looks like heaven on earth."

"Like Jabalpur?" I asked.

"No, Jabalpur cannot compare. Nothing can compare." He pulled out a picture of Northern Pakistan from underneath one of the pages. The darker black ink splotched at the edges. I thought it was a picture of Europe like the ones I had seen in numerous books. I saw a man herding sheep amongst the giant mountains wearing a grey shalwar kameez.

"Abu, is this what Pakistan looks like?"

"Not where we are going, but yes Zahida, this is our Pakistan. It has snowcapped mountains and springs of turquoise freshwater. And the greenest grass that doesn't grow like that anywhere else in the world. I read so many accounts of explorers describing this part which borders Afghanistan, and it sounds unreal. These parts have enough fresh water to supply the entire Pakistan if they form proper water lines." He showed me another map on which he drew out the water systems that could be made. My eyes widened.

I saw our reflection in the passing train. Abu had a pen above his ear. We sat on the dirty ground of the platform. He used the pen to scribble more little notes in brown journal. His black mustache now showed greys. The gash on his forehead left a purple bruise oozed with a yellow puss. We looked poor. We were poor. I wondered if this was what was in store for us,

poverty.

As the morning call of prayer brought upon dawn. Abu laid out Ami's shawl as a prayer mat on the platform and stood to pray. Many other men did the same following him and in a matter of minutes as far as the platform stretched men lined up shoulder to shoulder behind my father to pray. With a strong voice he led hundreds of men into their morning prayer.

"*Allah-u-Akbar.*"

Everyone knelt down with their foreheads touching the ground at the same time and in that moment, I saw my father richer than he had ever been. *Oh, how proud Ami would have been if only she could have seen this sight!*

Last Train

From Delhi
to Mirpurkhas, Pakistan
Duration: 14 Hours

Our money made its way into the pockets of men with full bellies and a badge appointed by the Indian government. Every stop, every train, and every boarding cost Abu his savings. They knew time was running out for us all and they took advantage of it. A single woman with an infant was trying to board the train.

"Show me your ticket," a man with a thick mustache and wearing police uniform said. He was a Muslim. She showed him their tickets.

"Where are you going?" The policeman asked.

"Mirpurkhas officer," the woman replied.

"There is no more space on the train."

"But I have a ticket officer." She explained.

"There is no space...unless you have something to offer. Money isn't the only currency I accept." The policeman sneered.

She brought her dupatta over her chest. A snarl grew from underneath his mustache.

"I don't have any more money on me. My child hasn't eaten for two days now. All I could afford were these tickets. Please, I need to board the train. I have two sons that are already in Pakistan." The train engine warmed up with a screech.

I rushed to Abu. He helped an elderly couple sit down beside Dadi.

"Abu they won't let a lady on the train. She has a small child. Can we do something to help them?" Abu got off the train and started questioning the man.

"What is the problem here?" Abu said.

"Who are you?" The policeman questioned.

"I am her brother."

"You didn't tell me your brother was on the train," the policeman said and turned to the woman.

"I...I..." The woman trailed off.

"Do you have no shame?" Abu's voice boomed. The man turned bright red.

"Watch my shame. Watch what I'll do to your so-called sister," he spat.

Abu grabbed him by the collar.

"You'd have to walk over my dead body first before you hurt any woman on this train."

The train charged forward and the woman

with her wailing child moved into the train. Abu yanked the policeman's collar with force. The fat policeman fell on his back.

"Pakistan will be free of rats like you. You are a shame to your own country," Abu bellowed and got on the train.

As the train rode out of Delhi, I saw the man beating a young boy working as a chai delivery worker.

The Camps Of Khokhrapar

Nothing was worse than the camps. After we took our last train out of Delhi to the border of Pakistan, we had to walk the rest of the way. There were camps set up along the way. We trudged with a band of hundred other immigrants. We were led by a few men who took handfuls of money with the promise that we would get to the other side. It was nothing like the picture Abu had shown me, there was nothing but desert. Endless hot scorching desert that burned our heels. It made our skin peel like garlic. There wasn't enough water. There was no water.

There was this woman amongst us. Her hair was long and black, and her skin was a beautiful deep golden color compared to the rest of us. She spoke Bengali. None of us understood her. She shouted Arabic words all day. I tried to calm her down on the first night. I sat beside her patting her back and holding her hands.

"*Yawm al-qiyamah*--the day of judgment is coming! The day of judgment is coming!" She kept repeating. I tore small pieces of dried bread and soaked them in a watery lentil soup and fed them to her.

"Do you have any family?" I asked her in Urdu and patted her back.

"The day of judgement is coming! The day of judgment is coming!" She yelled.

I didn't know what else to do. I invited her into our camp. Eventually she drifted into sleep curled up like a cat.

"I can call her *khala*, my aunt." I said to Dadi that night.

"Kurash is watching you right now from the sky. She is proud of you Zahida."

It was the longest five nights of our lives. We rested in the nights and marched in the day. I held the Bengali woman's hand and made sure she didn't get left behind. The desert grew cold at night. We wrapped Dadi in all the fabric we had. Her cheeks become hollow in our week-long train journey.

"Walk!" A man yelled in the day to all of us. "Walk! Or you won't make it and the border will close and you will die in this heat! These sand dunes will become your resting beds." So, we marched on tired, hungry, and thirsty from one camp to another. Abu had to carry Dadi most of the way. I took turns carrying Zubeida and Banu. The desert was never ending.

It was the last night before our final march to the border in the morning. We all huddled around a fire. It torched to the sky. In the dark sand all sorts of creatures slithered and gnawed underneath our feet. Dadi squinted at something in the distance.

"Water, there's water there!" She shouted.

There was no way there could be water. Everyone told Dadi to be quiet. I brought her back inside the tent and stroked her hair.

"Zahida, I am so cold. I need water," she whimpered.

"Dadi, there is no water left for the day. Tomorrow they will hand out more. I promise I will get you water first thing in the morning."

"Zahida, please my sweet beti I need some water."

I went back out to the fire to ask if anyone had any water.

"Do any of you have any water left?" No

one was willing to share.

A tall young dark-skinned man came up to me. "I was keeping it for my mother to take her medicine, but you can have it." I felt bad that he thought it was for me.

"It's for my Dadi. She is ill."

"I was studying medicine in Delhi before we left. I can take a look at her if you want?" I led him into our tent. He examined her eyes and pulse.

"She's been ill the whole journey; her fever won't break. It was too dangerous to stop for a doctor. We have been putting turmeric in her water," I explained.

He lifted her neck, and she took small sips of the water. Her lips peeled and lost colour. Her skin became yellow. He stroked back her white curls. Then he came up to me, leading me out of the tent.

"I am afraid she won't make it," he said.

"What do you mean?"

"She has something that doctors are calling influenza. It's not diagnosed yet or anything, but a lot of people have been passing away from it and a wave of it is predicted to come in the near future."

"She will make it. She will. You aren't even a real doctor. Just because you got to study in Delhi doesn't make you God." I crossed my arms and furrowed my eyebrows.

"I am sorry. I don't mean to make you upset. I just wanted to be honest with you."

"I don't need your honesty. I can see she is sick, but she will make it."

"We don't have enough water to hydrate her. If we want her to make it, we have to act fast. Maybe a doctor in Pakistan could help her."

"Zahida..." Dadi whimpered from inside the tent. We both rushed to her.

"I need clean fabric, anything? And some sort of other cloth to clean her. Just show me everything you have to eat also," he ordered.

He ripped apart one of my cleaner dupattas. He wrapped the sand that had gone cold into little bundles. He placed them over her forehead and on the heels of her feet.

"This will get her fever down." From his own tent he grabbed a sack of his own things. He used a small tool to crush some dried *tulsi* leaves and coriander seeds that he had in his sack along with a handful of other herbs. He put them in the water. Dadi chugged the water.

"Slow down. Please. Small sips. These herbs will help her body penetrate the water."

I was amazed. Dadi looked a little less yellow.

"Make her eat something, anything every thirty minutes." I nodded at his instructions. He stepped out of the tent.

"Here are some more tulsi leaves." He handed me the rest of the bundle that was in his sack.

"What if you need them?" I asked.

"Not more than your Dadi needs them."

"Thank you and I am sorry about what I said."

"My name is Shafi, call for me if you need me again." He disappeared into the night.

It was near dawn when Dadi started to shake violently. I told Abu to call for Shafi. Abu came back into the tent thirty minutes later.

"No one has seen him or his mother, they

are saying he might have left with another band of immigrants that marched through the night." Abu and I held Dadi's hand. She stopped shaking.

"Zahida, beti." She opened her eyes.

"Yes Dadi, I am here."

"Look, we made it," she said,

"We made it to Kurash's Pakistan. We made it to our Muslim land. Oh, that Kurash! I miss her so much. Your mother was the strongest willed woman I knew. I get to die on my land. On the land of Muslims. What an honour. I get to die for Kurash's dream."

"You aren't dying. You can't leave us too." All my little siblings gathered around her in that tent.

"Take care of our Pakistan," she said.

We all sobbed around her.

And when dawn did approach and the land was once again visible, we realized that Dadi had been right, there was water. The border was only a few hundred yards away, but at night it wasn't visible. Everyone's hearts lightened as they saw clay huts, people, wells, and palm trees. Water was close. We buried

Dadi at the border. She lay at rest in that desert, with nothing but miles and miles of Indian desert on one side and the village of Mirpurkhas Pakistan on the other.

The first well was only a few yards away. The Bengali woman ran towards it.

"Khala no! Wait, you might get in trouble." I ran after her. She reached the water and poured bucket fulls over her face. She cupped her hands and took big gulps. Others followed her. But before they could reach the water she started choking. White foam flowed out of her nose and mouth. Her eyes turned back. She fell into my arms.

"What's happening to her? Khala, Khala you will be okay." I patted her cheeks.

"They poisoned the wells. The Hindus," the man leading us said.

I stared up at the sky, the desert burned underneath my skin, and I sat there holding Khala's lifeless body to my chest. No tears, no words, just an endless sea of questions. *Why God, oh why?*

We have undoubtedly achieved Pakistan, and that too without bloody war, practically peacefully, by moral and intellectual force, and with the power of the pen, which is no less mighty than that of the sword and so our righteous cause has triumphed.

- Quaid-E-Azam Muhammad Ali Jinnah,
Founder of Pakistan

Chapter Eleven
Pakistan

It never rained here. The air was heavy, hot and sticky. It could suffocate a person. We stayed at our uncle's house until we could get a place of our own. The government promised equivalent housing to the one we left behind in Jabalpur. Every morning Abu combed his hair, ironed his white shalwar kameez, and grabbed his wallet and stood in the scorching sun for eight hours in front of the government buildings. Every evening he returned with disappointment and another task he needed to get done to claim his identity and wealth.

For the next three years I saw him get up every morning and try again. He got a small job at the newspaper press. Not to write

The Custard Apple Tree

because those kinds of jobs were taken by the people who were born on the land; the true Pakistanis. It all stopped making sense and I just spent the days working in the kitchen, doing laundry and biting my tongue at the comments my aunt and uncle made,

"When do you think they will leave?" Aunty asked.

"He's my brother, you know I can't just ask him to leave," Uncle said.

"Yes, you can, and you should before I do. It's been three years. That chai delivery job of his doesn't even make enough to feed the stray cats." I kept kneading the dough.

"Look he's not even home most days and Zahida has practically become our maid. Do you know the costs of maids nowadays?" My uncle tried to justify our stay everyday.

"You and your niece. I saw her poke her nose in your books, I bet you she's a thief like her mother was before she married that rich brother of yours. Where did all his wealth go anyways? I heard he left it all to some Hindu."

Tears trickled down my cheeks.

I missed my mother. I missed Ram Kaka.

And I missed my home.

I got a job tutoring at the local school. They were right that all children would have access to education in Pakistan. But it was no way for a child to learn; no chairs, no desks, no pens, and no books. Most of the teachers were not educated themselves. Most of the classes went by with the children playing and running around with no one to supervise them. I spent the little money I made buying pens. I asked Abu to bring home all the scrap paper he could get his hands on. I gave them lessons on Islamic literature; Galib, Rumi and Hafiz. They learned the Urdu alphabets and eventually they wrote their own poems.

Every night when I got home, I found Abu sitting on the front steps of the house.

"Why are you still up?" I asked.

"Who else do I have to share my day with?"

"Hmm. Let me think what about...that brother of yours?"

"You mean your uncle," he teased right back.

"Yeah, well he is not as much my uncle as much as he is your brother," I teased him.

The Custard Apple Tree

He pulled something out from behind him, it was a little bag.

"What is this?" I asked.

"Look inside."

I slid the material out of the bag. It was a new shalwar kameez. It was a dull orange with little sparkles.

"I love it...But this must have been really expensive, Abu."

"Now your Abu isn't that poor that he can't buy his daughter a new dress," he said.

"I didn't mean it like that. Thank you very much. I love it. I'll save it for Eid."

"No, you won't, you will wear it tomorrow. I'll get you a new one for Eid. What would your mother say if she saw the way you dressed? You alternate between two white dresses. One of which has a hole." I covered the hole on the bottom of my kameez with my hand.

"And no jewelry whatsoever. Zahida, you are young. I promise there is a beautiful life written for you."

"I know..." I went inside the house and fixed two plates of lentils and rice. I brought them back out to Abu.

"Let me guess you didn't eat either?" I asked. We both sat outside on the stairs under a sky of stars laughing about my aunt's angry face, discussing politics and eating our simple meal.

A little boy came running into my class.

"Are you Zahida *baji*? It's your father--" The chalk dropped from my hands and the air to my lungs stopped. I ran through the streets of Karachi that day. I ran as fast as I could. I couldn't lose him too. I couldn't. I raced through the narrow alleyways behind the little kid. My new dusty orange shalwar kameez was splattered with dirt when I finally got to the printing press. A group of men huddled around someone panting on the floor. I pushed them aside and made my way to Abu. His chest tightened. Abu had a lump the size of a lime in his throat.

"Someone call the hakeem!" I yelled. I cupped his neck with my hands.

"Abu you will be okay. You will be okay."

One of the Muslim Punjabi writers made their way over to the commotion.

"Who's creating all this noise? Take it outside! We have work to get done!"

"It's my father, something is happening to him. Can you please help us?" I whimpered at him from the floor.

"What does your father do here?"

"He delivers chai all day to the workers."

"Are you a *muhajir*?"

"What's that?"

"An Urdu speaking Indian immigrant."

"I am a Pakistani." I knew who I was.

"Were you born here?"

"This land was India as well before, no? What difference does it make where we were born? Wasn't it just a few years ago your father stood on this land proudly calling himself an Indian? An Indian today. A Pakistani tomorrow. What does it matter? Who knows the third day could be in your grave?" It was my mother that spoke from within me that day.

"You, You there. You dark skinned muhajir." He snapped his fingers at the skinny man carrying a tray of chai and a towel flung over his shoulder.

"Yes sir."

"Don't just stare at me! Throw this man and his daughter outside," he barked. Then he turned to me.

"And when your father does get better, that is if he gets better, tell him he was replaced by another dark-skinned muhajir."

"Keep your job and when you stand before God on the day of judgment tell him your birth pride got in the way of helping a dying man," I spat the words out between clenched teeth. I was so close to his face that I could smell his stale cigar breath.

I dragged Abu out with the help of the little boy. I picked him up by his shoulders and waved for a cycle rickshaw on the road.

I paid the hospital bill with one of my gold earrings. I paced back and forth in the foyer of the hospital, prayed my evening prayer on the floor, and pleaded for the health of my father. Late into the night the doctor came out of the operating room. Abu was diagnosed with throat cancer.

The Custard Apple Tree

I scrubbed the dirt and sweat out of my new dress on the rooftop. Abu soaked up the sun on his pale body.

"Eat more of that paan of yours! Great one more thing: your father has cancer. Chew more tobacco. In fact, I'll buy you some tobacco, you know what, I'll start eating it too! Then we both can be sick."

He giggled from behind a newspaper.

"Oh, this is funny to you. Also, you don't have a job anymore either. Thanks to us being Indian immigrant Pakistanis whatever that means you got fired. Fired! Now the little respect we did have in front of that brother of yours we don't have that either."

Abu laughed.

"Is this funny?" I grabbed the newspaper and asked with my arms crossed.

"No, I am just imagining you carrying me to the hospital. That is a funny sight. You and all five feet of you carrying me." He chuckled.

My anger simmered down, and my lips lifted into a smile. I plopped down by his feet.

"God, what will I do with you Abu?"

"How did you carry me?" He kept laughing.

"All I can say is that you've gotten fat, old man."

He chuckled some more.

"Now we are poor, and I am an old fat man with sickness. I wonder what your aunt will have to say about that."

I did her best expression,

"Now that the old man is crippled, I say we poison his tea and send him off for good." We both laughed.

Chapter Twelve
The Necklace

Months passed. One day, a mailman with letters spilling out of his tote bag rang our doorbell.

"Does a Syed Murad Ali live here?" The mailman asked.

"Yes, that's my father."

"Is this his house?"

"No, this is his brother's home."

"I am going to need his signature."

"He is actually really ill; can I sign in his place?"

Minutes later I ran into Abu's room waving the letter.

"Abu there's a letter for you." I called out to him as he slept on the floor of the small room buried under old wool blankets.

"A letter?"

"Yes, a letter, maybe our request got approved and they gave us something to live in of our own."

"To die in a home of my own, that would be a gift from God."

"How about living in your own home, that would be a gift from God to us."

"Read the letter. What does it say?" I crinkled open the folded pages.

"Abu this isn't from the government officials. This is from Ram Kaka!" Abu used his arm to prop up against the cold wall.

"Ram?"

"Yes Abu, Ram Kaka. It's from Ram Kaka. It's from Jabalpur! From home." A smile spread across both of our faces.

"Show me Zahida, let me hold it." He held the paper, grazed the words with his fingers, and hugged the letter to his chest.

"Read it Zahida. Tell me what it says. My eyes can't see these words anymore."

Dear Murad,

My brother. I hope this letter finds you well.

"Wait before you start reading. I have to tell you something," Abu interrupted.

"You know I left everything to Ram, right? The house, the business, every penny. There was no way to bring it here. He didn't take it, but he said he would guard it till the day we returned."

"Abu, you don't have to explain. Ram Kaka was our family. There was no way to bring that wealth over. I am glad it went to someone we know rather than just some stranger." Still a spur of jealousy tingled in my heart.

I hope this letter finds you well. I wish I could ask with a certainty of a reply how the children are? Is Zahida married? How's your mother? What is Pakistan like? But I am not even sure if this letter will reach you. They have finally allowed the two countries to have some exchange. Write me a letter as well. I am guarding your home still. I go once a week and have it cleaned for your return. I don't want to live in it, it's your home. There are no more Muslims left in Jabalpur. The mosque was torn down and is being turned into another temple. The years have been long. I am healthy and my family is doing well. We all miss you. Bhavna is married now and has a son who is a year old. I wanted to ask if you still have what I gave you? I wanted to remind and assure you that I have taken care of that just how you told me to for all these years. I will safeguard your home until the day I die. Remember me in your prayers. In the envelope are some jasmine flowers from your garden. I thought the smell of home would bring comfort. I miss you brother. I miss you more than you can imagine. Everyday is harder without you by my side.

In my prayers,

Ram.

I pulled out the handful of flowers from inside the envelope. They turned pale over the long journey. I brought them up to my nose and for a moment I was back home. My chin trembled and a tear trickled down my cheek. I placed them in Abu's hands. He did the same and closed his eyes.

"They smell like her... like, Kurash." His hands shook as he placed them in his kameez pocket along with the small jewelry box full of the dirt from her grave that he always kept on him. A dim light seeped into the room from the setting sun outside. It lit the dark damp room with its grey concrete walls.

"What did Ram Kaka give you Abu?" I asked. "That day at the train station, what did he put in your hand?"

"It was this," Abu pulled out a chain from the bag of dirt. On the end of the chain was a dainty small gold coin.

I took it into my own hands. I knew where it was from. I had seen it around Aarav's neck.

"Where did you get this?" I asked.

"Off of that boy's neck. The boy on our front steps. The night I went to Ahmedabad." He didn't have to remind me.

"Why do you have it? Why do you carry it around like a trophy? Is it some sort of keepsake of Hindu blood?" I cried out.

"Zahida. What are you talking about?"

"You ignored that boy. You ignored his death. Abu, he doesn't...even have a headstone. Did he even make it back to his family? Did he get cremated like all Hindus do?"

"You think I stuffed dirt in his mouth?" Abu asked.

"I think that there is a lot about that night which was buried in dirt. He was innocent Abu."

"I saved the pendant for you. I found it on dangling from one of the doors rails."

"For me?"

"Yes, for you."

"Why?"

"I thought you'd want it, just like the little box of dirt I keep in my pocket. I gave it to Ram to keep until we left so no suspicion aroused. Ram returned the boy's body to his family. He got a proper Hindu ceremony. I left a fund for his family. I don't know why he died on our steps, and I didn't know if he ..."

"If he what?"

"Did he try to hurt you? I knew Zahida, everyone knew you adored him."

I poured my heart into telling him about the glass of water, the festival, the night, the men and finally how he died. The soft light turned into a silver moonlight by the time I was done. I felt lighter. I felt like my secret was finally out and finally I laid Aarav to rest. Abu listened and nodded.

"It wasn't your fault. You couldn't help him even if you wanted to. And you might have helped Zahida if it weren't for you having to protect your own family. You have to forgive yourself."

"I just have this feeling, like I could have done something, anything." I melted into Abu's arms.

"No, Zahida my sweet daughter, you did everything you could have. You survived. We both did. Life hasn't been kind to my sweet daughter and I couldn't be prouder of the person you have become."

"Abu, can we put the necklace in the sea? I want this to be the end of it."

"Tomorrow we can go to the sea."

As Abu sunk into a deep sleep, I sat in the moonlight braiding my hair down my back. I held the necklace up in the silver light. All these years had passed but somehow the past made its way back. I wonder how many more ghosts I still had to see before this haunting was finally be over.

Zahid took a day off of school to take us to

the sea. I needed his help to carry Abu into the cycle rikshaw. He didn't mind but I didn't want my brother missing a day of school. But this was important. I had never seen the ocean. In all these years we never found the time to explore our own city. It was beautiful; soft white sand, salty sweet clean air, and the blue roaring waves. Vendors sold spicy corn on the cob, samosas, and coconut water.

I took out some bills from the end of my dupatta and asked Zahid to grab anything he wanted. His eyes lit up. He had turned into a young man himself; with broad shoulders and my mother's soft features. I protected him; I protected all of them from the nightmare we lived through. They found a way to preserve their childhood through it all and for me that was enough.

"Go with him," Abu said.

"Me?" I asked.

"Yes, go I don't mind sitting here in peace. I need it. I will watch you guys. Go touch the water."

"I'd look silly Abu."

"You're twenty years old, not forty. Go be

young." I took off my sandals and dipped my toes into the water. It felt warm and tingly on my feet. I giggled. Zahid raced up beside me. He rolled up the bottom of his shalwar and set down the snacks beside Abu.

He rushed into the water splashing me with the waves.

"Zahida watch out!" Zahid yelled. A big wave of water swamped my way and I landed on my feet soaked from head to toe. Abu and Zahid both laughed.

I pushed Zahid into the water and his outfit got wet too. Then Abu and I laughed at him. The sun felt warm when we finally came out of the water. We sat beside Abu on the warm sand, sipping coconut water and munching on hot corn as the orange fiery sunset dipped over the light blue waves. A thin crescent moon appeared on the other side where the sky was already a midnight blue. And slowly a splatter of stars twinkled on the beautiful pallet as well.

"You ready?" Abu asked me as Zahid went to grab a cycle rickshaw.

"I am ready." I slipped the necklace off

my wrist where I had tied it like a bracelet. I flung my arm and threw the necklace into the endless sea. A new life, a better life awaited me.

That night when Abu slept, he didn't wake up the next morning.

My uncle and aunt closed the door on us. The little boy who led me to the printing press was the only person I knew in the whole city. He led me again, *this time to the huts.*

The Present

Karachi, Pakistan
Year 1951
Five Years After the Partition

What is meant for you, will reach you even if it is beneath two mountains. And what is not meant for you will not reach you even if it's between your two lips.

   - Imam Al-Ghazali, 11th Century Mystic

Chapter Thirteen
The End

It's the night before my wedding day. I have no idea who I am marrying. I don't want to get married but I have little say in the matter.

My uncle arranged it. We only see them on big holidays now and that too briefly. One day he showed up at the door of our small hut, demanding to see me.

I welcomed him in. I asked him to take a seat on one of the two straw beds all nine of us share for the past two years. He refused to sit. He paced back and forth in the little space.

"You are getting married," he ordered. I dropped the steel spoon I was using to stir the chai.

"What?"

"You are getting married."

"Why?"

"What do you mean why? You are at a proper age and as your father figure that responsibility falls on me." Uncle said. Father figure--the word sounded like a joke. Abu was his father for all his life; he raised him, fed him, educated him and now that same brother left Abu's kids to eat stale bread dipped in warm water for dinner.

"I can't get married," I said.

"What do you mean? You're a girl. If you don't get married what else will you do?"

"I have to take care of my siblings."

"Do I not take care of you guys? Is that what you are implying?"

Two visits a year and a handful of rupees every month that were the sum of a beggar's day wage wasn't the care we needed. But he was all we had. All my siblings had. I looked at my sisters still lost in their imaginary childhood world.

"Yes, you do take care of us. I am very grateful. I meant around the hut there is a lot to do. Like the cooking and cleaning."

"Your aunt and I know what is best for you. You are getting married. They will learn how to take on the responsibility once it falls on them. I remember you running around in that big garden of your father's. Now look, he died, and you took on some real-life responsibilities, didn't you?"

The words stung. I swallowed the giant lump in my throat.

"I will see you at the wedding," he said.

All I could manage to do at that moment was open the drape of our hut to show him the way out. Uncle turned to me, scoffed and left.

Now the straw bed digs into sore muscles. All the holes in the fabric over our hut suddenly start to become visible like staring at the night sky. Sleep will not come tonight. I slap away mosquitoes from my bare skin. The oil in the lantern finishes and the light goes out, leaving the hut pitch black. I slip on my sandals and refill it with more oil. My siblings huddle on the two beds; curling into one another.

I hold the lantern over it over the old steel suitcase in which we keep all of our belongings. I plow through fabrics, dishes and books throwing things left and right. And there it is buried under everything; the lace red dupatta that I grabbed from Ami's closet the night we left. I peer at myself in the broken shard of mirror set overtop a wooden chair with taped legs.

I pull my hair back into a low bun, apply a thin layer of lipstick and lay the red dupatta atop like a veil. The person staring back at me is my mother. I look just like her. But my naseeb isn't anything like my mothers. I have nothing. I am nothing. This world has given me nothing but pain. This marriage will just bring more.

I use the rest of my old dupattas to sew small patches to cover the holes into the hut's drape. I work the night away with a needle and thread in my hands and an oil lamp set beside me, but a thought keeps festering in my mind; *what if that night I ran away with Aarav?*

"This is Zubair Chacha. He used to be a soldier back in India. I want him to attend my wedding today Uncle." They briefly interact with each other at the steps of my uncle's mansion.

"Go on in Zahida, your aunt will help you get ready upstairs," Uncle says.

"I have one request," I ask him. "I want jasmine flowers in my hair. Can you get me some?"

He rolls his eyes but before he can speak Zubair Chacha interferes.

"There is time before the ceremony. I'll go get them for you, beti," Zubair Chacha says.

My dress is a simple pink with silver beading. My hair is laid back into a low bun. Silver jewelry shimmers around my neck, ears, ankles, nose, wrists and hair. My cheeks and lips are rosy. The henna on my hands turned into a dark burgundy. Zubeida brings up jasmine flowers and Ami's red dupatta folded neatly on a silver plate.

After everyone has left the room, I sit there on the chair against the vanity staring at myself. A new life awaits me downstairs. A tear of sadness, fear, hope and longing trickles down my cheek as I lace the jasmine flowers around my bun. If only Abu and Ami were beside me. I imagined my wedding to be grand, fit for a princess in my childhood. Oh, how life has humbled me. Some years ago, if you told me my own story I would have laughed. But the lessons of life are unpredictable.

I place Ami's dupatta over the sheer pink one covering my face. Banu and Zubeida walk me down the steps. Banu brought Barfi. The white cat purrs at the end of the staircase. I keep my head down. My stomach churns.

I see a silhouette of a man seated on one of the two chairs set out for us. Even though he is sitting, he appears tall. He wears a black *sherwani* on which goes down to his knees and a white pajama underneath. A rose garland dangles around his neck. I take my seat beside him. The mullah recites the wedding ceremony. He repeats the question three times. "Do you Muhammad Shafi lawfully take Zahida Begum as your wife?"

"I do." A man's deep voice replies.

"Do you Muhammad Shafi lawfully take Zahida Begum as your wife?"

"I do."

"Do you Muhammad Shafi lawfully take Zahida Begum as your wife?"

"I do."

Then he asks me the same question. My shaky voice complies.

Someone hands him a mirror. My muscles tighten. *This will be the first time I see my husband.* He places the mirror underneath my dupatta. A familiar face glances back at me. We both recognize each other instantly. Shafi from the camps of Khokhrapar. Another ghost from the past, this time a friend.

His dark hair and eyes compliment his Southern Indian golden skin tone. Now he even has a mustache like a grown man. His eyes aren't framed with circles this time, he looks rested.

He has beautiful almond eyes batted with a thick coat of curly eyelashes. I quickly glance away from the mirror. We sit alone in the room as it empties out of people leaving to enjoy the wedding lunch. The room fills with an awkward silence. Shafi adjusts his rose garland over and over again. He wiggles around his feet and tugs his collar every now and then. Somehow that eases my own set of nerves and I finally end the silence.

"Did you finish becoming a doctor?" I ask

He clears his throat. "No, I couldn't get into any of the universities. All the spots were reserved for--"

"The people born on this land."

"Yeah. They said I was a--"

"Muhajir."

"Yeah."

"How's your Dadi, did she make it?" Shafi asks.

"No, she didn't. She um, passed away that morning."

"Oh, I am so sorry."

"It's okay. It feels like it was a long time ago. Almost feels like a past life to be honest."

"I know what you mean."

I didn't know anything about him but somehow, I knew Shafi had his own set of nightmares that tormented him.

"I was actually adopted when I was a kid, I found out about my birth parents right before the partition. They couldn't make it across the border in time," he says.

"Oh. I am so sorry. My mother's grave is in India."

"All my real family is there too. I got a job working on the trains to see if I could travel back and forth."

"My father passed away too with cancer a few years after my Dadi."

"I am sorry," he replies.

"Look at us two young people who just got married and this is our first conversation." I chuckle.

"It is strange for sure, but our lives have been strange. Hey, maybe it was all for this moment."

Blush rushes to my face.

"Do you live in one of the huts?" I ask.

"No, I live in a small house. I bought it myself. I live there all alone. Walls, kitchen and a bathroom. The whole package. And now it's yours, all of it. And the cats'." He lifts Barfi. She licks his knuckles. I can't help but

The Custard Apple Tree

almost jump with excitement. A real house.

"And your siblings...if you accept it. All I have craved for these long years is a family. I don't want to be alone anymore." His smile brightens the room and after years I feel the warmth of the sun again and not its burn.

I am stunned at his generosity. I feel a guilt creep in for how I never shared anything with anyone when I had so much.

"That's very, very kind of you."

"You're my wife now, it's my job and plus I see how your sister's been tearing up all evening. The partition took me from my family. I would never do that to a family."

Now all the sudden, I am the one fiddling with my dupatta. It's all overwhelming. I feel so much. The question in the sand that I asked God that day has finally been answered.

Shafi interrupts my thoughts, "And I also have an outside area in front of my house."

"Really? You have a garden?"

"You couldn't call it a garden. More like a strip of land that I know nothing about taking care of. It has only one tree. The neighbors told me it's a custard apple tree. Do you know what that is? It's green from the outside. I think it's a plant, I don't think you can eat it."

"Yes. Yes, I know what that is. We had hundreds of them at my home. They are fruits. I can't believe it; you have a custard apple tree. A custard apple tree."

"It's yours now."

I shy away.

I had to lose everything to learn the value of one single custard apple tree.

⌣

I sip on a warm cup of chai. The winters have been cooler these past few years.

"Amma!" I hear Zubair crying outside in the garden. I put away my book and run outside. I lift him up into my lap. I wipe the dirt off of his elbows. Barfi purrs at the bottom of my shalwar.

"How many times have I told you not to climb the tree?"

"But Amma look." He lifts up a small custard apple cupped in his hands.

"I picked it for you."

I kiss his little nose that's already taken the hooked shape of his fathers. He grabs at the jasmine flowers in my hair.

I lost one more person in the last seventeen years of my marriage; my daughter. She was two years old. A wicked illness took her away from us.

"Don't climb the tree! Ask me and I'll get it for you," I scold him and tap his hand.

"Okay sorry Amma," he pouts. I let him down and he runs around the garden. He hides behind the rose and jasmine bushes.

Shafi comes out of the house.

"What's all the commotion?" He puts his hand over my shoulder, I lock my fingers with his.

"This isn't even commotion. That will be tomorrow when all the cousins get together at Banu's house."

"Glad we aren't the ones supervising that."

We watch Zubair as he runs around. The cold touches the tips of our noses turning them pink. The evening sulks deeper and the sky turns into a beautiful midnight blue. A little star twinkles above us and I know Abu and Ami watch over us.

Pakistan gave me the noor of my eyes;

Shafi and Zubair and for that I am grateful. I trusted God and he gave me a life that I'd do it all over again for. Their love finally melted the snow.

Glossary

Abaya: Long black dress

Allah Hafiz: Go in the protection of God

Allah-u-Akbar: God is great

Api / Baji: Sister

Beti: Daughter

Diya: An oil lamp made from clay

Dupatta: A long scarf

Hakeem: Doctor of Islamic Medicine

Halwa: A sweet Indian dessert

InshAllah: If God wills

Jai Hind: Long live India

Jihad: A struggle or effort in the way of a righteous cause

Jummah: Friday

Jaan: Life

Kurta: A long loose-fitting collarless shirt

Kyun Faya Kyun: Be and it is reference to the Quranic verses

Lungi: A garment wrapped around the waist and extending to the ankles

Muhajir: Urdu speaking immigrant

Mullah: A Muslim priest

Naseeb: Destiny

Nikah: Islamic marriage

Noor: Divine light

Paan: Betel Leaf

Pyari: Lovely

Qawali: Sufi devotional music

Rangreza O Rangreza: The one that paints colors

Rikshaw: A three-wheeled public conveyance

Salam: Peace be upon you

Sari: Long garment draped around the body

Shalwar Kameez: Loose trousers and tunic top

Sherwani: A long-sleeved knee-length coat

Tulsi: Holy Basil

Ustad: Teacher

Acknowledgments

Firstly, I want to thank Allah. All credit is due to the divine.

Alhamdulillah for the life I live today and for making my biggest wish of becoming a writer come true. He truly is merciful and everlasting. It's through Allah's love this book came to be. I am eternally grateful.

Thank you to Professor Allen for believing in all of us when the journey of making a book was killing us. Thank you for not giving up.

I cannot even begin to thank all the people that said kind words about my writing. To all those who read my silly short stories and told me I had a talent that could result in a book someday. Thank you for your words, they hold the most special place in my heart.

Thank you to my writing friends and readers. Without you it wouldn't have been possible. Your words of encouragement made me believe in myself so much that I wrote a whole novel.

Thank you to my sister Aleeza who will always

go to war for me and who has pulled me out of my darkest times.

To Rayan for making me laugh when I was buried under endless stress.

To Yousuf for being the older brother I always wanted.

To Yahya, my biggest blessing and the noor of my eyes. I love you kid.

To Mama for taking care of me when I stayed in my room all day writing.

To Baba who I owe my entire life to. My pillar, my foundation and the strength I wish to carry throughout my life. Thank you for working day and night and sacrificing your own dreams so I could live out mine. I promise to work hard and make you proud.

And of course, my friends, Sidra, Zayna and Noorma. Thank you for reading everything I write.

And lastly, my childhood and the books that made it the most magical place. I owe it to Geronimo Stilton, Goosebumps and A Series of Unfortunate Events for filling my childhood with colours. Books have been my escape and it is truly an honour to have the gift of writing.

Alhamdulillah, Rafiqa

Manufactured by Amazon.ca
Bolton, ON